HARRAP'S

Tests anglais

par
Brigitte BUIRE

HARRAP

Edition publiée en France 1991
par HARRAP BOOKS Ltd
43–45 Annandale Street
Edinburgh EH7 4AZ
Grande-Bretagne

© *Chambers Harrap Publishers Ltd* 1991

Tous droits réservés. Toute reproduction intégrale
ou partielle, faite par quelque procédé que ce soit,
est soumise à l'autorisation préalable de l'éditeur.

ISBN 0 245 50119 3

Réimprimé 1995

Imprimé en Grande-Bretagne par
Clays Ltd, St Ives plc

PRÉFACE

Les **TESTS ANGLAIS** traitent de l'essentiel de la grammaire anglaise, offrant ainsi un moyen d'auto-apprentissage et d'auto-évaluation. Cet ouvrage s'adresse à toute personne qui dispose déjà de bonnes connaissances de base : les élèves du second cycle des lycées, les élèves des classes préparatoires, BTS et IUT, les étudiants non spécialistes et quiconque souhaite renforcer ses connaissances et remédier seul à ses difficultés.

L'apprentissage autonome est facilité par une approche progressive et par les corrigés en fin d'ouvrage. L'authenticité de la langue est toujours respectée grâce à des extraits judicieusement choisis dans des publications anglo-saxonnes. Certains aspects de la langue américaine sont discrètement présents afin d'élargir le champ culturel de l'utilisateur.

Le nombre et la diversité des exercices proposés, les scores après chaque test pour évaluer son niveau, permettent un travail précis et efficace.

Conseils d'emploi et évaluation

Une étude suivie ou une consultation ponctuelle du livre est possible. Cette dernière est facilitée par un index alphabétique qui mentionne les termes grammaticaux, les mots-clés et les éléments anglais ou français traités dans l'ouvrage.

Le score obtenu à chaque test permet de mieux connaître son niveau. Il est tout à fait normal de ne pas toujours obtenir un bon score dès le premier essai. Si un test ou tout un chapitre

vous pose trop de problèmes et si malgré le corrigé, des points obscurs subsistent, nous vous conseillons de vous reporter à votre outil de travail habituel (grammaire, manuel) et de reprendre le test ou le chapitre en question après un certain temps.
Si votre score
- se situe entre 90 et 100 % : vos connaissances sont excellentes ;
- se trouve entre 80 et 90 % : votre niveau est bon ;
- se situe entre 60 et 80 % : votre niveau n'est pas mauvais mais nous vous recommanderions de refaire le test ou le chapitre après un certain temps et de revoir éventuellement le point précis dans une grammaire ;
- est inférieur à 60 % : ne soyez surtout pas découragé, travaillez tranquillement le point faible à l'aide d'une grammaire et refaites les tests plusieurs fois si nécessaire.

Nous vous souhaitons bon courage, des progrès en anglais et beaucoup de plaisir en travaillant avec ce livre.

TABLE DES MATIÈRES

1. L'ARTICLE — 9
   - A. L'article indéfini — 9
   - B. L'article défini — 10
   - C. Article défini ou indéfini ? — 12
2. LE NOM — 15
   - A. Le pluriel des noms — 15
   - B. Les suffixes — 17
   - C. Les noms composés — 19
   - D. Les noms de nationalité — 21
3. LA POSSESSION — 23
4. L'ADJECTIF — 27
   - A. La place de l'adjectif — 27
   - B. Les degrés de comparaison — 27
   - C. Les adjectifs composés — 29
   - D. Les adjectifs de nationalité — 31
   - E. Les préfixes — 31
   - F. Test récapitulatif — 32
5. LE PRONOM — 35
   - A. Pronoms réfléchis et pronoms réciproques — 35

B. Les pronoms relatifs	37
6. LES QUANTIFIEURS	40
7. L'ADVERBE	47
8. INFINITIF ET GÉRONDIF	51
9. LE PRÉSENT	59
10. LES TEMPS DU PASSÉ	62
11. LE FUTUR	70
12. LE CONDITIONNEL	73
13. LES AUXILIAIRES MODAUX	77
A. Formes simples	77
B. Formes composées et équivalents	79
C. Tests récapitulatifs	83
14. LES VERBES COMPOSÉS	85
15. LES REPRISES VERBALES	91
A. Les « Question-tags »	91
B. Les « Tags » de réponse	93
16. LES QUESTIONS	97
17. LES STRUCTURES VERBALES	101
A. Les causatifs : « Faire faire »	101
B. La proposition infinitive	104
C. Structures idiomatiques avec inversion	106
D. Tests récapitulatifs	107
18. L'EXCLAMATION	111
19. LE PASSIF	113

TABLE DES MATIÈRES

20. LE DISCOURS INDIRECT	117
21. LE GROUPE VERBAL : RÉVISION GÉNÉRALE	123
22. LES PRÉPOSITIONS	129
A. Les prépositions de lieu	129
B. Autres prépositions	130
23. LES MOTS DE LIAISON	135
24. LES NOMBRES	140
25. HANDLE WITH CARE !	142
A. To make - To do	142
B. To say - To tell	145
C. Les faux-amis	146
26. AMÉRICANISMES	150
CORRIGÉS	155
LISTE DES VERBES IRRÉGULIERS	203
IDIOMES ET PROVERBES	212
INDEX	220

1. L'ARTICLE

A. L'ARTICLE INDÉFINI

a) Complétez ces phrases par l'article indéfini a ou an.

(1) ... igloo is the house of (2) ... Eskimo.
What (3) ... interesting article I read in *Time*.
You can't make (4) ... U-turn here.
Do you know what (5) ... MP is ?
It took them (6) ... hour and (7) ... half to pack their luggage.
(8) ... few years ago he married (9) ... Chinese girl.
Do you think he can find (10) ... better job in (11) ... urban area ?
They finally found (12) ... room for the night in (13) ... YMCA.
She does look good in (14) ... one-piece swimsuit.
His father was not (15) ... honest man, to say the least.
Do you mind wearing (16) ... uniform to go to school ?
Do you spell "exercise" with (17) ... "S" or with (18) ... "C" ?
She does too many things at (19) ... time and is always in (20) ... hurry.

score : ... × 5 = ◯

10 L'ARTICLE

b) Complétez ces phrases par a, an ou ∅ (pas d'article).

How long did you work as **(1)** ... advertising executive ?
Christmas will be on **(2)** ... Monday this year.
Is there **(3)** ... room for me in the car ?
It's difficult to find so efficient **(4)** ... man.
Why don't you clean up the garage ? It's in **(5)** ... terrible mess.
(6) ... great patience is necessary when bringing up children.
He left his farm to go the city to find **(7)** ... work.
The house they bought is **(8)** ... real beauty !
Never have I been to such **(9)** ... fantastic opera !
Victor Hugo was both **(10)** ... poet and **(11)** ... novelist.
He has **(12)** ... dinner out twice **(13)** ... week.
Have you made **(14)** ... appointment with the dentist ?
Orson Welles, **(15)** ... American film director, was also **(16)** ... oustanding actor.
How can anyone live on $ 500 **(17)** ... month ?
There used to be **(18)** ... huge iron-works here.
What **(19)** ... pity you didn't come to the party, it was great **(20)** ... fun.

score : ... × 5 = ◯

B. L'ARTICLE DÉFINI

a) Complétez les blancs par the ou par ∅.

Do you think **(1)** ... green suits me ?
(2) ... Dad always cooks **(3)** ... breakfast on **(4)** ... Sundays.

(5) ... Chinese venerate (6) ... old age.
(7) ... President De Klerk was elected in 1989.
They'll be living on (8) ... 12th floor.
Was she born on (9) ... 5th of March too ?
(10) ... cancer kills fewer people every year than (11) ... car accidents.
(12) ... ''Crisis'' is an organisation that helps (13) ... poor and (14) ... homeless.
(15) ... California's state capital was named after (16) ... Sacramento River.
(17) ... elephant is (18) ... earth's largest mammal.
In France (19) ... museums are closed on (20) ... Tuesdays.

score : ... × 5 = ◯

b) Complétez les blancs par the **ou par** ∅.

It is said that (1) ... life begins at 40.
(2) ... tea is just warm water to me.
It was nice seeing (3) ... good old George again.
(4) ... skateboarding can be dangerous at times.
Millions of people watched (5) ... Prince Charles's wedding on (6) ... TV.
(7) ... Queen always finds (8) ... time for her passions :
(9) ... horses, (10) ... racing and (11) ... country life.
They went trekking in (12) ... Himalayas on (13) ... lower slopes of (14) ... Mount Everest.
She studied (15) ... Russian history at (16) ... university.
Stalin was (17) ... leader of (18) ... Soviet Union when (19) ... US entered (20) ... World War II.

score : ... × 5 = ◯

L'ARTICLE

C. ARTICLE DÉFINI OU INDÉFINI ?

a) Complétez ces phrases par a, an, the ou ∅.

Why don't you send for **(1)** ... doctor if you have **(2)** ... temperature and **(3)** ... sore throat ?
In **(4)** ... 1950's **(5)** ... McCarthyism was **(6)** ... blatant manifestation of **(7)** ... American intolerance.
(8) ... Germans think that **(9)** ... speed limits could reduce **(10)** ... pollution of their forests.
(11) ... most industrialized countries have to come to grips with **(12)** ... problem of **(13)** ... pollution.
Could **(14)** ... ban on **(15)** ... ivory trade help save **(16)** ... elephants in Africa ?
(17) ... Alps attract **(18)** ... crowds of tourists in **(19)** ... summer.
(20) ... French are very proud of **(21)** ... Concorde.
(22) ... yen is **(23)** ... Japanese currency.
(24) ... Mississipi has its source in **(25)** ... Minnesota.

score : ... × 4 =

b) Compléter ces phrases par a, an, the ou ∅.

Can you travel everywhere in Europe without **(1)** ... passport ?
(2) ... man loves making **(3)** ... war but is afraid of **(4)** ... death.
Why did he choose to play **(5)** ... cello of all things !

Why don't you take (6) ... aspirin if you have (7) ... headache ?
(8) ... whole family enjoys playing *Pictionary*.
(9) ... honesty, (10) ... efficiency and (11) ... ability of (12) ... English bobby has always inspired (13) ... admiration abroad.
(14) ... estimated 300,000 people marched on (15) ... US capital (16) ... last week.
Are you (17) ... believer in (18) ... death penalty also called (19) ... capital punishment ?
Prince Philip, (20) ... Queen Elizabeth's husband, is at (21) ... head of (22) ... WWF, (23) ... biggest organization of (24) ... protection of (25) ... nature.

score : ... × 4 = ◯

c) **Complétez ce texte par** a, an, the, **ou** ∅.

(1) ... President has (2) ... passion for (3) ... history and is obsessed by his place in it. But he also has (4) ... great respect for (5) ... history. He has always had (6) ... passion for (7) ... foreign policy. He devours (8) ... history books and collects (9) ... maps of (10) ... world. As (11) ... young deputy at the end of (12) ... forties and in (13) ... early fifties, he was already talking ardently about (14) ... need for (15) ... construction of (16) ... united Europe and (17) ... importance of creating (18) ... Paris-Bonn axis. As (19) ... leader of (20) ... Socialist Party in opposition he made (21) ... point of touring (22) ... globe and meeting (23) ... foreign heads of state and government ; and during his

eight and a half years as **(24)** ... president his penchant for **(25)** ... foreign travel has by no means diminished.

score : ... × 4 = ◯

d) Traduisez ces phrases en évitant le mot à mot.

(1) Avez-vous du feu ?
(2) Brossez-vous les dents tous les jours !
(3) Un jour tu comprendras !
(4) Tu m'as sauvé la vie !
(5) Il a serré la main du président.
(6) Il a le mal du pays.
(7) Rentrons à la maison.
(8) Il n'y a pas besoin de se dépêcher, nous avons bien le temps.
(9) Le repas est prêt, à table !
(10) Faites le plein, s'il vous plaît.

score : ... × 10 = ◯

2. LE NOM

A. LE PLURIEL DES NOMS

a) Mettez les mots en italiques au pluriel.

Put your (1) *brush* in the (2) *box* under the (3) *bench*.
I often give (4) *scarf* as presents.
In France (5) *mouse* are supposed to bring presents to (6) *child* when they lose their (7) *tooth*. In America (8) *tooth-fairy* do.
Are there any active (9) *volcano* in this area ?
The Muslim religion allows (10) *man* to have several (11) *wife*.
I can't get used to tissue-paper. I much prefer (12) *handkerchief*.
Why are (13) *woman* discriminated against ?
These (14) *machine* only work with (15) *penny*.
We walked so much, my (16) *foot* are killing me.
We were very impressed by the two (17) *grand-piano* on the stage.
Can you see those slate (18) *roof* over there ? It's the new housing development.
To make foie gras (19) *goose* are force-fed.
He came back from school with his head covered with (20) *louse*.

score : ... × 5 = ◯

16 LE NOM

b) Mettez tous les mots possibles au pluriel.

(1) *The Wales* Charles and Diana are not very often seen travelling together.

(2) *Tiger* as well as (3) *elephant* are endangered (4) *species*.

She was told never to contradict (5) *grown-up*.

When under-developed (6) *country* move towards more (7) *equilibrium* and (8) *equality,* the former (9) *have-not* will evolve into (10) *have*.

All the (11) *tennis-fan* are closely following the (12) *up and down* of French Open winner Michael Chang.

These are the (13) *basis* you must start working on.

Remember "aggressive" is spelt with two (14) *"g"* in English.

(15) *Wallet* or (16) *purse* are often recovered because (17) *thief* mostly look for (18) *cash*.

You're wasting your time, he never listens to (19) *advice*.

He didn't fell like socializing with the (20) *University people*.

Many (21) *M.P.* resent having their (22) *session* televised.

What's for dessert ? (23) *Fruit* ?

It's often said that (24) *woman-driver* drive more carefully than their male (25) *counterpart*.

The teenager stopped several (26) *passer-by* and asked them for cigarettes.

Throughout history, people have been persecuted for their religious (27) *belief*.

Can you give me 50 (28) *penny* to buy sweets, Mum ?

He never feels at ease with his (29) *brother-in-law*.

They were charged with the robberies of several (30) *savings-bank*.

score : ... × 10/3 = ◯

LE NOM 17

B. LES SUFFIXES

a) Complétez les phrases ci-dessous par un substantif dérivé du mot en italiques en utilisant les suffixes.

-ee -ism -er -ment -ette -hood -ness -tion -ful -ist

(1) A ... writes *novels*.
(2) When you boast of being *clever*, you are proud of your ... .
(3) When you go to the cinema, the girl who *ushers* you in is an ... .
(4) The quantity your *mouth* can contain is a ... .
(5) To *cook* your meals you need a ... .
(6) You live in a nice ... if the area around your house is attractive and your *neighbours* are decent people.
(7) If you retire from regular ..., you are no longer (8) an ..., you are no longer *employed*.
(9) A ... is a phrase or a passage you *quote* from a book, a play or a poem.
(10) The economic and political system of *capitalist* countries is known as ... .

score : ... × 10 = ◯

b) Même exercice. Opérez les transformations nécessaires.

-th -cy - ism - ess -dom -(e)ry -ty -ial -er

(1) When a journalist *criticizes* the policy of the government, he voices ... .

LE NOM

(2) Being *miserable* is referred to as ... .
(3) If you are an *efficient* person your asset is ... .
(4) The act of *denying* something is ... .
(5) When you are *poor* you're in a state of ... .
(6) If you are a *wise* person you must act with ... .
(7) If it takes you a *long* time to convince somebody, then you've gone to great ... .
(8) The man who *waits* on you in a restaurant is a ... but (9) the girl is a ... .
(10) You buy *jewels* in a ... store.

score : ... × 10 = ◯

c) Complétez les phrases par un substantif dérivé du mot en italiques en utilisant un des suffixes proposés. Opérez les transformations nécessaires.

(1) Napoleon had three sons, not one of whom lived to *mature*.

-ation / -ity / -ness / -ing

(2) In many African countries people are threatened with *starve*.

-ness / -ity / -ation / -ism

(3) He reached *man* but never once did he act as a man.

-kind / -dom / -hood / -ship

(4) Every year thousands of muslims make the *pilgrim* to Mecca.

-age / -dom / -ity / -ation

(5) Alcoholics are people propelled towards *drunken*.
    -ness / -ing / -hood / -ism
(6) The *illiterate* rate in the USSR is the lowest in the world.
    -ation / -cy / -ism / -ness
(7) "The proper study of *man* is man".
    -ship / -hood / -kind / -dom
(8) Our bridge club was very successful in its *member* drive.
    -ing / -ment / -age / -ship
(9) Contrary to all *to expect* he finished his work on time.
    -ation / -ancy / -ment / -ing
(10) He always tries to escape the *weigh* of his responsibilities.
    -al / -t / -th / -ing

score : ... × 10 = ◯

C. LES NOMS COMPOSÉS

a) Complétez par un nom composé.

(1) At customs you show your passport to the ... .
(2) When you have a hard time going to sleep, you can take a ... .
(3) Water that you can drink is ... .
(4) If you don't like to do the dishes you can always get a ... .

(5) You record your favorite TV programmes with a … .
(6) Everybody must pay taxes to the … .
(7) When you want to know what the weather will be like, you listen to the … .
(8) Camping is not authorized here ; there's a … two miles down this road.
(9) Someone who is politically on the right is a … .
(10) More and more people use a … to cook food quickly by electromagnetic radiation.

score : … × 10 =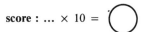

b) Même exercice.

(1) A pupil that leaves school or college before he or she has finished his/her studies is a … .
(2) Someone who is lazy and never does anything well is a … .
(3) His father was an engineer and hoped his son would be an engineer too, thus following in his … .
(4) Another well-known expression referring to the common man or the average Joe is … .
(5) Before or after you have a bath you can wear a … .
(6) A flight of steps can also be called a … .
(7) The wife of your father by his second marriage is your … .
(8) …, often shaped like a pig, are used by children to save money in.

(9) When you have pleasant thoughts about things you would like to happen, you have ... .
(10) But if these things are impossible in reality, utopian, then they are ... .

score : ... × 10 = ◯

D. LES NOMS DE NATIONALITÉ

a) Remplacez le nom de pays en italiques par le nom de nationalité.

(1) *Great Britain* are not used to shaking hands.
(2) *Portugal* used to be great colonists.
What are the inhabitants of *Denmark* called ? (3) ... .
(4) *Puerto Rico* and (5) *Mexico* make up an important percentage of the American population.
(6) *Greece* are very proud of their past and their culture.
Most (7) *Germany* are very satisfied with the reunification of their country.
In recent years a lot of (8) *Vietnam* and (9) *Cambodia* have left their countries for the West.
A lot of Jews around the world wish to emigrate to Israel and become (10) *Israel*.

score : ... × 10 = ◯

b) Remplacez le nom du pays en italiques par le nom de nationalité.

When communicating with foreigners it is important to be aware of the various interpretations different countries give to certain hand gestures.

For example, when a **(1)** *Poland* slaps his forehead with an open hand, he usually means : "you're crazy". On the other hand, when a **(2)** *Great Britain*, a **(3)** *Scotland* or a **(4)** *Spain* taps his forehead, it is meant as an expression of self-praise.

Similarly, if a **(5)** *Holland* raises his index finger while tapping his forehead, it means the person is clever.

For the **(6)** *Finland* as for the **(7)** *Sweden*, a wagging finger might signify mild disapproval, a threat or be used merely to emphasize what they are saying.

For the **(8)** *Japan* the traditional meaning of the rounded, pinched-thumb and index-finger is "money". But for the **(9)** *Norway* this same gesture has an offensive or obscene meaning.

In Islamic countries, the left hand has a sinister reputation and consequently, when dealing or shaking hands with an **(10)** *Iraq* for example, one should only use the right hand.

score : ... × 10 = ◯

3. LA POSSESSION

a) Choisissez la solution qui convient.

(1) Observing traffic rules is every **motorists / motorist / motorist's / motorists'** responsibility.

(2) In the past decade interest in **women's rights / woman rights / woman's rights / women rights** has been on the decrease.

(3) **The Moscow Mc Donald's / The Moscow's Mc Donald's / The Moscow's Mc Donald / The Moscow Mc Donald** is the largest of the company's 11,300 restaurants.

(4) A typical meal costs about five rubbles which is half **the wagesday / a wagesday / the day-wages / a day's wages** for a Soviet worker.

(5) **Andy and Jesse's / Andy's and Jesse's / Andy's and Jesse / Andy and Jesse** chances for graduation are good.

(6) He was now working on a biography of **S. Lewis life / S. Lewises' life / S. Lewis-life / S. Lewis's life**.

(7) He worked for a while at **his uncle's grocers' shop / his uncle's grocer's shop / his uncle's grocer shop / his uncle grocer's shop**.

(8) Certain principles of government were laid by the Founding Fathers in **the United States's constitution / the United States constitution /**

LA POSSESSION

United States' constitution / the United-States-constitution.
- (9) Honesty is **this man / the man's / the man / this man's** main quality.
- (10) In this old photograph, Father appears as a young lieutenant in a **World-War-II-uniform / World War II uniform / World War II's uniform / World War II uniformed**.

score : ... × 10 = ◯

b) Même exercice.

- (1) **Societies institutions and values / Society-institutions and values / Society's institutions and values / The society's institutions and values** haven't yet adjusted to the new roles of women.
- (2) The flight was late and an **hour's delay / hours' delay / hour-delay / delay-hour** had just been announced.
- (3) Because of the changes in the benefit system made by the Thatcher government, **16-and-17- year old / 16-and-17 years olds / 16-and-17-year- olds / 16-and-17 years old** do not get assistance from the government today.
- (4) Television invites people to be passive. To switch on is an easy way of excusing oneself from going anywhere and working in **one's / its / one / ones** garage.
- (5) Why don't you sit at the table next **of hers / to herself / to her table's / to hers** ?

LA POSSESSION

(6) We are expected at **the Osborne's / the Osbornes' / the Osborness's / the Osbornes' family**.

(7) This book is a creditable attempt to make science understandable to **the street-man / the man-in-the-street / the men in the streets / the street's man**.

(8) "To your health and a very happy birthday to you", he exclaimed holding his glass **at arm length / at arms' length / arm-length / at arm's length**.

(9) The article about Japanese imperialism in **last week's *Financial Times* / last-week- *Financial Times* / last weeks' *Financial Times* / last week- *Financial Times*** was most controversial.

(10) After **the Wright brother- flight / the Wright brothers' flight / the Wright's brother's flight / the Wrights brother's flight** it was widely believed that before long there would be flying machines for everyone.

(11) **For God-sake / For God sake / For God's sake / For Gods' sake**, make him stop that racket.

(12) Her hair was the same colour as **her mother's / her mother-hair / those of her mother / her mother's ones**.

(13) In 1979, Margaret Thatcher became **British / Briton's / Britain / Britain's** first woman prime minister.

(14) Her policies are not based on some economic theories but on things she and millions like her were brought up with : "an honest ... for an honest ...". (**day-work - day-pay / day's work - day's pay / day work - day pay / workday - paid day**)

(15) He has a passion for hunting and owns a superb

collection of **deer's antlers / deers' antlers / deer-antler / deers-antlers**.
- **(16)** Their divorce was as much his fault as **his wife's / his wife / to his wife / of his wife's**.
- **(17)** He fears **his parents reaction / his parents' reaction / his parent's reaction / his parents-reaction** when he comes home late.
- **(18)** KLM is supposedly **the world-1st-airline / the world 1st airline / world's 1st airline / the world's 1st airline**.
- **(19)** Don't let your dog walk into **baker's / bakery-shop / the baker's shop / the bakers' shop**.
- **(20)** These two businessmen are to meet in **the nation's capital / the national capital / the nation-capital / the nations' capital**.

score : ... × 5 = ◯

4. L'ADJECTIF

A. LA PLACE DE L'ADJECTIF

Remettez les éléments en ordre de façon à reconstituer des phrases cohérentes. Attention à la place des adjectifs.

(1) furnished / lived / spacious / he / in / restored / a / five-room / apartment / in / New England / a / house / scantily

(2) angular / tall / man / he / worn / features / a / with / is / balding / middle-aged

(3) yellowed / he / shake / presented / headmaster / the / dirty / to / with / gnarled / a / hand

(4) has / single / his / past / every / never / before / years / ten / working / eight / day / left / he / office / the / in

(5) paned-windows / warm / long-slung / large / 's / welcoming / Island / building / Ellis / of / air / a / main / today / surprisingly / red / and / has / brick

score : ... × 20 = ◯

B. LES DEGRÉS DE COMPARAISON

a) Transformez les adjectifs en italiques en utilisant le degré de comparaison qui convient.

She used to be much (1) *thin* before she had her baby.
The Soviet Union is the World's (2) *large* oil producer.

The traffic is **(3)** *heavy* today than last week-end.
Even **(4)** *radical* youths are likely to grow conservative when they acquire power and prosperity.
Europe is said to be **(5)** *polluted* continent, but Africa is becoming **(6)** *habitable*.
The relationship between humanity and its environment is a subject of **(7)** *great and great* concern in developing countries.
Samuel Johnson wrote that "dictionaries are like watches ; **(8)** *bad* is **(9)** *good* than none, and **(10)** *good* cannot be expected to go quite true".

score : ... × 10 = ◯

b) Même exercice.

Infant mortality is said to be **(1)** *high* in the US than in some **(2)** *affluent* societies.
Who, do you think, suffers **(3)** *much* in periods of inflation ?
As a reporter he was always given **(4)** *tough* foreign assignments, where the fighting was **(5)** *fierce*, and the living **(6)** *hard*.
She is **(7)** *much* uninterested in your problems ; why continue to bore her with them ?
In her **(8)** *late* book, I believe that Alison Lurie is at her **(9)** *fine*, even though some detractors don't find it **(10)** *well-written* her previous works.

score : ... × 10 = ◯

c) En utilisant l'amorce proposée, reformulez les phrases, sans en changer le sens.

(1) If the negative is perfect, the print will be good.
The more ...
(2) There weren't as many mistakes in your essay this time as last time.
There were ...
(3) German video recorders are more expensive than Japanese ones.
Japanese video recorders are ...
(4) His short-stories are better than his poetry.
His poetry is ...
(5) I can understand Italian better than I can speak it.
I can't speak ...

score : ... × 20 = ◯

C. LES ADJECTIFS COMPOSÉS

a) Transformez les phrases en remplaçant les éléments en italiques par des adjectifs composés.

Charlie Brown is forever in love with (1) *a little girl with red hair*.
She was born in (2) *a family socially above the middle-class*.
People sometimes think that America is (3) *a complacent nation whose only centre of interest is itself*.
The window of their lodge-room looked out onto a superb view of (4) *Kilimanjaro which is 19,321 feet high*.
He was of opinion that writing advertisements was no job for (5) *a budding poet who had respect for himself*.

30 L'ADJECTIF

Miriam Makeba, **(6)** *a singer who was born in South Africa* hopes to return home after living through **(7)** *an exile which has lasted three decades*.

He calls everything from purple to black **(8)** *very dark blue;* he must be **(9)** *incapable of distinguishing colours*.

Nothing really affected him and he always went around with **(10)** *an attitude of "I couldn't care less"*.

score : ... × 10 = ◯

b) Complétez ces phrases par un adjectif composé.

(1) The French TGV which travels very fast is a ... train.

(2) A problem that has existed for a long time is a ... problem.

(3) What do you call the famous London red buses ? ...

(4) A tradition that has been honoured for many years is a ... tradition.

(5) A film that is not recommended for people under the age of 18 is an ... film.

(6) Today if you have a serious heart-problem it is possible to undergo ... surgery.

(7) Someone who is easily angered is ... .

(8) If a thief is caught in the act of robbing, he is caught ... .

(9) When you can't afford a brand-new car, you have to settle for a ... car.

(10) She can't find clothes her size in department stores, she has them ... at an expensive tailor's.

score : ... × 10 = ◯

D. LES ADJECTIFS DE NATIONALITÉ

Remplacez le nom du pays en italiques par l'adjectif de nationalité.

Hong Kong is the undisputed capital of **(1)** *China* cooking.
(2) *Switzerland* clockmaking is famous all over the world.
In 1963, **(3)** *the Soviet Union* Valentina Tereshkova was the first woman in space.
Unlike most other languages in Europe **(4)** *Finland* and **(5)** *Hungary* languages are not Indo-European.
Green is the **(6)** *Ireland* national colour.
Hercule Poirot, the short, snobbish **(7)** *Belgium* detective is Agatha Christie's most popular character.
Would you care for a piece of some **(8)** *Denmark* pastry ?
At the end of my street, there's a **(9)** *Pakistan* grocer who stays open until 12 o'clock.
Hordes of tourists have posed for photos standing under the 19-foot sign of the **(10)** *Wales* railway-station of Llanfairpwllgwyllogerychwyrndrobwllllantysiligogogoch.

score : ... × 10 = 〇

E. LES PRÉFIXES

Complétez ces phrases en ajoutant un des préfixes suivants aux adjectifs en italiques :
-dis / -un / -im / -in

Don't stare at people like that, it's **(1)** *polite*.
Our holiday in Cyprus was a very **(2)** *pleasant* experience.

Why do you feel so **(3)** *satisfied* with your life these days ?

She is a very **(4)** *balanced* child, **(5)** *capable* of doing anything right.

Her opinion on the subject is quite **(6)** *partial*.

He always has the most **(7)** *believable* stories to tell us.

Her sons are **(8)** *patient* **(9)** *contented* young men.

It's the most **(10)** *comfortable* bed I've ever slept in.

The flat they rented when they were in London was quite **(11)** *expensive*.

I've lost again. How **(12)** *lucky* !

His teenage daughter is becoming more and more **(13)** *agreeable*.

I refuse to do business with such a **(14)** *honest* person !

Don't you find it **(15)** *convenient* to live far away from everything ?

Your approach to the problem of homelessness is both **(16)** *realistic* and **(17)** *fair*.

There must be something wrong with him. He sounded **(18)** *pleased* on the phone.

Many women still complain about **(19)** *equal* pay.

If you refer to someone as a "louse", you mean they do nasty and **(20)** *honourable* things.

$$\text{score : ... } \times 5 = \bigcirc$$

F. TEST RÉCAPITULATIF

Choisissez la solution qui convient.

(1) When would you like me to start on the job?
Sooner better / Soonest best / The soonest / The sooner the better.

L'ADJECTIF

(2) Both these dresses look nice on me, but I prefer **the fanciest / the fancier one / the fanciest one / fancier one.**

(3) Every year, basketball attracts **millions / millions of / million / million of** spectators in the US.

(4) In spite of the fact that he was able to explain rationally almost every phenomenon of ... he was afraid of .... **(the supernatural - dark / supernatural - dark / the supernatural - the dark / the supernatural - the darkness)**

(5) Who was **the eldest / the elder / the older / oldest** of the Brontë sisters ?

(6) **Italy people / Italians / Italy's people / Italian** always cook spaghetti "al dente".

(7) Over the piano was printed a notice : "Please do not shoot the pianist. He's doing **his better / the best / best / his best.**"

(8) Coke is the planet's most popular soft drink, with **600 million of / 600 millions / 600 millions of / 600 million** servings sold daily.

(9) If things go well, we should be able to cater **not far / nothing less but / no fewer than / not short of** 100 meals a day.

(10) He finally decided to change his life-style altogether **for the best / for the better / for best / for better** I hope !

(11) Should **the homeless / homeless / the homeless people / the homeless' people** be given more assistance from the government or should they be left to look after themselves ?

(12) Mr Riley is about **48 years old / 48-year-old / 48 year's old / 48 years** I would guess, very tall, with thinning brown hair.

34 L'ADJECTIF

(13) Several ... people died and several ... became ill after the industrial disaster of Bhopal in India. **(thousands - hundred of thousands / thousand - hundreds of thousand / thousand - hundreds of thousands)**

(14) In this Chinese restaurant the choice of teas is as important **than / as / that / Ø** the choice of wines is in a French restaurant.

(15) ... men live, ... they become. **(longer - wiser / the longest - the wisest / the longer - the wiser / the longer - as wise)**

(16) The very **less / least / last / lesser** you could do is send him a birthday card.

(17) This summer, forest fires are **all the more devastating as / more devastating because / the most devastating because / all the more devastating that** it hasn't rained for quite a while.

(18) They live in an old, secluded, wind-blown house on the coast of Maine, but they are **not the worst for it / none worst for it / not any worst for it / none the worse for it.**

(19) Bill and Paul both thought they could manipulate each other, but in the end it was Paul who had **an up hand / the uppest hand / the upper hand / the upper hands.**

(20) In London, an estimated 50,000 **young / young people / the young / of young people** aged 16 to 19 have taken up residence on the streets for want of a home and job.

score : ... × 5 = ◯

5. LE PRONOM

A. PRONOMS RÉFLÉCHIS ET PRONOMS RÉCIPROQUES

Choisissez le pronom qui convient.

(1) Let me have your coats and make **you / yourselves / yourself** comfortable.
(2) Between **ourselves / the two of us / each other** I don't think much of his paintings.
(3) He still dresses **himself / Ø / by himself** like the yuppie he used to be.
(4) Everyone at the fair enjoyed **himself / themselves / oneself** very much.
(5) Adolescence is often a period during which the young revolt **themselves / itself / Ø** against their parents and society.
(6) Don't worry, the house is big enough so that you needn't get in **each other's / each other / one another** way.
(7) They met **Ø / themselves / oneself** during their junior year in high school.
(8) She can't understand why these two long-standing friends stopped seeing **him / themselves / each other.**
(9) They started arguing about nuclear disarmament and ended up calling **each other's / themselves / each other** names.

LE PRONOM

(10) God helps those who help **themselves / them / onself**.

(11) The flat I rent is very nice but the thing is, I'd like to have one **of mine / of my own / of myself**.

(12) She didn't like living **all to herself / all by herself / all herself** in this big house.

(13) All things considered, the advantages and disadvantages balance **each other / themselves / them** out.

(14) How could she have let **herself / oneself / themselves** become involved with such a man ?

(15) The countryside around Chapel Hill is very nice ; Chapel Hill **by itself / for itself / itself** is a charming town.

(16) "Does your leg hurt ... ?" - "Yes it does, I hurt ... when I slipped on those wet leaves." **(you - Ø / Ø - myself / yourself - me)**

(17) She resented the idea of her friends' matchmaking. She could take care of her social life **herself / to herself / for itself**.

(18) One should trust no one but **themselves / oneself / himself**.

(19) After his two weeks' holiday he felt **him / Ø / by himself** a new man.

(20) "Should I ask this girl out or not ?" - "Well, I can't answer that ! You have to work it out **yourselves / for one another / for yourself**."

score : ... × 5 = ◯

LE PRONOM

B. LES PRONOMS RELATIFS

a) Complétez les phrases avec le pronom relatif qui convient.

I don't want anyone to tell me **(1)** ... to vote for and **(2)** ... my political convictions should be.

His mother insists on taking him to art exhibitions, **(3)** ... he finds boring.

Scholarships are given to students **(4)** ... parents have a very low income.

He is a man **(5)** ... enjoys good conversation and dislikes women **(6)** ... talk is merely gossip.

Make up your mind **(7)** ... part of Ireland you'd like to visit.

(8) ... kids are learning at school should prepare them for the 21st century not for the 1950s.

He refuses to subscribe to a magazine **(9)** ... editor is anti-semitic.

Do you know the woman **(10)** ... is trying on that very becoming dress ?

score : ... × 10 = ◯

b) Choisissez le solution qui convient.

(1) I'm so confused I can't tell what's **which / of that / what**.

(2) Do you remember the time **that / where / when** I was working in a nuclear plant ?

(3) He was the least important member of the household, the one **who / whom / which** noone took seriously.

LE PRONOM

(4) Please pay attention to **that / which / what** you're doing.

(5) Can you tell me the reason **why / for what / which** lots of people are afraid of spiders ?

(6) The price of cocaine follows the same rules of supply and demand **that / what / who** apply to soybean or wheat.

(7) Iran has an estimated 2 million weavers most **of whom / whom / of those** are nimble-fingered young girls or women.

(8) All **Ø / which / that** glitters is not gold.

(9) Tourism is not the only problem ... plagues the Alps ... are affected by everything from acid rain to nuclear fallout. **(who-which / that-which / Ø - that)**.

(10) They live in a comfortable four-story chalet **of which / of whose / of whom** they rent out one floor.

(11) He was the kind of person **whom / whose / that** gossip always reached at least 5 months late, if at all.

(12) She was going to marry a musician, **what / which / that** was as bad as marrying a painter and probably worse than marrying a writer.

(13) **Which / What / Ø** little time he had left after his day's work, he would spend with his aged mother.

(14) **That / Whatever / Whenever** he will always come off best goes without saying !

(15) He lives like a tramp **who / that / which** he is.

(16) Today women **that / whose / of whom** own mothers probably didn't work, are entering the work force in large numbers.

(17) Having become suspicious, he had got into the

LE PRONOM 39

habit of coming home at irregular times to surprise his wife with **whomever / whoever / whatever** she might be.

(18) This is the most gripping baseball game **that / to which / where to** I've been to in years.

(19) **With what / What with / That with** the house to run and her full-time job, she hardly has any time left to herself.

(20) He behaves like the misogynist **who/so/that** he is.

score : ... × 5 =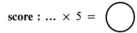

c) Traduisez en prêtant attention aux différentes fonctions de "dont" et "ce que, ce qui".

(1) Voilà ce dont j'ai besoin.
(2) Je ne connais pas le chef d'orchestre dont tu me parles.
(3) Ne pose pas de questions dont les réponses sont évidentes.
(4) Sa guérison dépend de la façon dont il va supporter ce nouvel antibiotique.
(5) Je n'aime pas la façon dont il me regarde.
(6) Pourquoi ne vas-tu pas chez le Docteur Eliot dont le cabinet se trouve à 5 minutes de chez toi ?
(7) Il a réussi son examen, ce dont il est très fier.
(8) Fais ce que je te dis.
(9) Elle disait toujours que son fils finirait par devenir un bon à rien, ce qui s'avéra être vrai.
(10) C'est une vraie perle ! Il répare tout ce qui ne marche pas dans la maison.

score : ... × 10 =

6. LES QUANTIFIEURS

a) **Complétez en utilisant** some, any, not, no, a **ou un de leurs composés.**

Is there (1) ... mayonnaise in the fridge ?
No, but there's (2) ... bottle of ketchup.
We met (3) ... very charming people last week.
It's a very difficult situation, I can see (4) ... way out.
He wanted to borrow (5) ... money from me, but I didn't have (6) ... .
The lights are out ; there's probably (7) ... at home.
He paid absolutely (8) ... attention to her.
Have you read (9) ... interesting lately ?
She's got (10) .. brother, but (11) ... sisters.
What's the name of this street ? I can't see a sign (12) ... .
"Would you like (13) ... cream with your coffee ?"
"No thanks. But I'd like (14) ... lump of sugar."
"Which one would you like ?" "(15) ... will do."
There was (16) ... mail for me today. There never seems to be (17) ... .
She doesn't eat (18) ... (19) ... more. She's on a diet.
Is there (20) ... left in the car ?
I'll be home tomorrow, drop in (21) ... time you like.
You can't learn (22) ... else's lesson.
I can't find my scissors. (23) ... must have removed them from my sewing-box.

Did you go **(24)** ... last night ?
(25) ... ever asks him his opinion.

score : ... × 4 = ◯

b) Complétez ces phrases avec un quantifieur :
much, little, enough...

(1) The idea that women are poor car drivers is not supported by ... real evidence.
(2) You said you liked to travel light. Why ... luggage then ?
(3) Except in Manhattan and in ... other city centres, there is hardly **(4)** ... public transport.
(5) ... American movies are complete without a high-speed car chase and **(6)** ... television shows seem to contain **(7)** ... else.
(8) Help yourself to ... fruit.
(9) You've spent far ... money on that hi-fi !
(10) I don't think ... of this budding author's first novel.
(11) In this school, on ... given day a quarter of the students are absent.
(12) She was lucky ... to get a ticket for the concert at the last minute.
(13) Julian is nicer than Brian in many ways and he knows ... more about music and literature.
(14) Van Gogh's paintings appeal to ... people because **(15)** ... academic or critical background is required to appreciate them.

42 LES QUANTIFIEURS

(16) Would you like ... dressing on your salad ?
(17) The USSR publishes twice as ... books every year as China.
(18) Under ... circumstances should children be allowed to play with matches.
(19) "Whom did you get as a baby-sitter ?" "... young high school girl who badly needs a couple of dollars."
(20) They only have one child but they think it is one ....
(21) She wanted to hire someone who could do ... of the cleaning as well as the laundry.
(22) There are ... people attending baseball games this year.
(23) I know I haven't been ... of a father lately but I'll make it up to you and take you to a movie this afternoon.
(24) She kept silent, telling herself that they would learn the truth soon ....
(25) Look at this sign, it says : ... parking, ... standing, ... stopping, ... kidding.

score : ... × 4 = ◯

c) Choisissez une des solutions proposées.

(1) This millionaire maintains three palaces costing $ 5 million in upkeep **all / most / several / each** year.
(2) I don't believe him any longer because I caught him lying on **either / fewer / several / every** occasions.

LES QUANTIFIEURS

(3) Although ... agrees that our planet is in danger, not ... feels the need to help fix it. **(neither of them-everybody / everyone-everybody / everyone-nobody / someone-all)**

(4) I found the last question the hardest in **the whole / all / any / many** test.

(5) She stays at home ... day listening to records. That's about ... she's been doing lately. **(the whole-whole / all-all / several-all / all-the whole)**

(6) Would like to go hiking or horseback riding ? I can make arrangements for **two / both the / ones / either.**

(7) Only one out of **all / the whole / both / every** five Asian Americans does not complete high school in the US.

(8) **All / The all / Both / Every** of our belongings, which we had left in the car, were stolen.

(9) He spent **most / few / each / little** of his life studying Indian culture.

(10) Conditions are difficult for **two / neither / every / both** students and teachers in our university system.

(11) **Every / Each / All / Whole** things considered, I'll give it a try.

(12) **Neither ... or / Neither ... nor / Either ... or / Neither of them ... nor** Fred ... John want to work on their father's farm.

(13) She is a very proud mother, **either / each / everyone of / both her** children completed medical school.

(14) An athlete needs to sacrifice **enough / all / no / everything** to become a star.

(15) He had **any / several / neither / too much** dollars left over from his January paycheck.

44   LES QUANTIFIEURS

(16) After their car accident **both their / anyone of them / neither of them / either of them** recovered from their severe injuries.

(17) In spite of efforts to prevent it, the Earth continues to be damaged and polluted **each / all / whole / some** day.

(18) It's a complicated story, I just don't feel like going into **all / many / the whole / most** thing right now.

(19) More than half of American students graduate from high school without studying **either ... or / neither ... nor / or ... or / either ... nor** world history ... western civilization.

(20) Since the US has no national system of health insurance for the entire population **the whole / most /some of / so much** Americans have private medical insurance.

score : ... × 5 = ◯

d) Même exercice.

(1) Is there **something / anything / nothing** wrong with you ? You look awfully pale today.

(2) I asked them whether Mr Scott was running for reelection, but **anyone / someone / noone** seemed to know.

(3) She wasn't **anywhere / somewhere / anything** near as pretty as her sister.

(4) She would have liked to own a car but couldn't afford **one / none / not one**.

(5) Of the thousands of Mexican illegal aliens that crossed the border last year **as many as / as little as / as much as** 800.000 were apprehended.

(6) One good turn deserves **other / another / the other**.

(7) People have realized that environmental problems are not .... They are .... (**somebody else-everybody / someone else's-everybody / somebody else's-everybody's**).

(8) **One / Some / None** but a fool squanders his time.

(9) Of his favourite writers, T.S Eliot, Hemingway and Faulkner are the modern **some / ones / other**.

(10) Some people believe in UFOs but I don't believe there is **any such / such one / another** thing.

(11) You don't look **too any / any too / some too** well today.

(12) She never wanted to be **anything other / something other / anyone other** than a housewife.

(13) She was annoyed when **anyone / another / noone** criticized her children.

(14) Larry and Tom went fishing yesterday, but ... caught ... (**neither of them-nothing / either of them-something / neither of them-anything**).

(15) Because of extensive poaching there are **more and more / fewer and fewer / less and less** elephants in Africa.

(16) In Japan **one / several / most** housewives' cooperative owns organic dairies and manufactures soap from recycled cooking oil.

(17) I have read several of Mailer's works, **none / no / any** of which I have liked.

(18) She had never earned money doing **neither / nothing / anything** except baby-sitting.

46   LES QUANTIFIEURS

(19) He leaped through the window with a crash. There was no **another / other / any** way of escaping the fire.

(20) The prospects of starvation, drought in Africa, man migration and social conflict are becoming **the whole too / all too / too little** likely.

score : ... × 5 =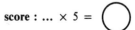

7. L'ADVERBE

a) Placez correctement l'adverbe en italiques. Evitez les structures emphatiques.

She had seen her before but didn't remember her (1) *really*.
I am pleased with my new car (2) *altogether*.
He is in a hurry (3) *always*. He does anything (4) *consequently* / (5) *rarely* / (6) *well*.
Some people believe that men and women have an unequal number of ribs (7) *still*.
There won't be room in the boot for all that luggage (8) *enough*.
Education was elitist (9) *still* / (10) *quite* / (11) *then*.
Among other things, he had been a car-salesman (12) *also*.
He does not smoke (13) *usually* / (14) *very much*.
Contrary to popular belief, very few people speak English (15) *still* / (16) *fluently* / (17) *nowadays*.
He brings her a dozen roses on Mother's day (18) *always*.
She ordered a drink from the waiter, but as he didn't come quickly, she became annoyed (19) *enough*.
I need a new tennis racket (20) *very much*.

score : ... × 5 = ◯

L'ADVERBE

b) Remettez les éléments en ordre de façon à faire des phrases cohérentes. Attention à la place des adverbes.

(1) holiday / now / we / on / will / any / be / almost / day
(2) intelligently / rather / talked / nevertheless / incessantly / she / but
(3) they / books / too / because / stopped / me / invariably / I / reading / made / much / think / completely
(4) have / week / club / a / usually / we / meetings / only / once
(5) warm / away / better / is / out / already / it / really / be / right / had / getting / you / off / ;

score : ... × 20 =

c) Réécrivez les phrases en plaçant l'adverbe ou l'expression adverbiale en début de phrase et en procédant à une inversion.

(1) He would never repeat my secret to anyone.
(2) She hardly ever feeds them greens.
(3) "I will tell you where my money is hidden under no circumstances", the old man said very quietly.
(4) He seldom socialized with the natives.
(5) You go up now, it's time for bed.
(6) I have never in my life met anyone as conceited as this man.
(7) He hasn't once told me he loved me in ten years of living together.

- **(8)** Two months had hardly gone by when her brand-new car broke down on the highway.
- **(9)** In his autobiography he does not refer anywhere to his children by his first marriage.
- **(10)** They went off loaded down with their camping-gear.

score : ... × 10 = ◯

d) Choisissez la solution qui convient.

- **(1)** How can I speak to him in Dutch, I **ever** / **hardly** / **rarely** / **still** know the language.
- **(2)** The summer we had was the hottest and driest **yet** / **still** / **whatsoever** / **already**.
- **(3)** As for me, she said, Prince Charming is **but** / **already** / **yet** / **hardly** to come.
- **(4)** Nobody **always** / **ever** / **often** / **never** asks him his point of view.
- **(5)** We hardly **never** / **always** / **sometimes** / **ever** meet.
- **(6)** He left his wife with three children, but what is worse **even** / **since** / **yet** / **still** he refuses to pay child-support.
- **(7)** He borrowed a large sum of money from his uncle but so **far** / **much** / **long** / **well** hasn't paid him back.
- **(8)** If you've done it once, you can do it **still** / **again** / **over** / **any more**.
- **(9)** He may have been married **before** / **still** / **ever** / **yet**.

L'ADVERBE

(10) This is the worst drought we've **still / never / ever / already** had in ten years.

(11) Have you **never / ever / once / always** seen the Concorde taking off.

(12) There is **again / still / any longer / ever** a lot of male chauvinism in England because of the single-sex educational system.

(13) "Have you ... had breakfast ?" "No, ...".
(already-not yet / already-not still / ever-again / still-never)

(14) Haven't you **still / yet / hardly / ever** noticed how often English people use understatements ?

(15) He **hardly always / hardly ever / hardly never / rarely hardly** goes out for lunch.

(16) He has no early classes, **and yet / similarly / therefore / on the other hand** he has time to eat a big breakfast.

(17) Bungee jumping is a dangerous sport, but people like dangerous sports ; so it is **here / always / still / again** to stay.

(18) She won't come back to Anna's house **sometimes again / again / no longer / ever again**.

(19) She doesn't know where she is going and if she will come back ; nobody cares **never / either / no more / neither**.

(20) He had **hardly some / yet any / hardly any / still none** energy left after the match.

score : ... × 5 = ◯

8. INFINITIF ET GÉRONDIF

a) Mettez le verbe en italiques à la forme qui convient : infinitif avec ou sans to ou gérondif.

(1) *to steal* ! A girl like that can't be a thief.
(2) Would you like me *to tell* you the story of Red Riding Hood ?
(3) It's no use *to grumble*, it's your own fault, you asked for it.
(4) I wish you would stop *to complain* about how untidy my place looks.
(5) Why did you make him *to think* you were a retired pilot ?
(6) I couldn't help *to feel* sorry for him.
(7) He claims he's totally incapable of *to learn* foreign languages.
(8) Most men would rather *to have* a son as their first child.
(9) There's something wrong with that furnace. It keeps *to make* a clanging noise.
(10) She lets them *to have* their way because she hates rows.

score : ... × 10 =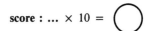

INFINITIF ET GÉRONTIF

b) Même exercice.

(1) I can't remember *to hear* that joke before.
(2) He was running so fast that he had to stop *to get* his breath back.
(3) I must remember *to bring* my books back to the library.
(4) Country people have a hard time *to get* used to
(5) *to see* highways (6) *to replace* rural roads and gas stations (7) *to proliferate*.
(8) It's not necessary for you *to go* to so much trouble.
(9) You can't expect me *to be* always at your beck and call, can you ?
(10) There are many reasons for *to admire* the female sex.

score : ... × 10 = ◯

c) Complétez à l'aide d'une des solutions proposées.

(1) Fancy **I paying / paying / I paid / pay** £10 for a tie I won't wear !
(2) Why **to grow / growing / grow / having grown** a beard ? You know you won't like it.
(3) They'd rather ... in Paris than ... their vacation on the Riviera in August. **(stay-spending / stay-to spend / staying-spending / stay-spend)**
(4) ... at a French person's house with a bouquet of chrysanthemums is tantamount to ... your hostess to drop dead. **(show up-tell / showing up-telling / show up-telling / showing up-tell)**

INFINITIF ET GÉRONTIF

(5) I wouldn't consider **to send / sending / to have sent / send** my children to a private school.

(6) His late working hours make it difficult **for him to have / for him having / for him to having / for having** much of a social life.

(7) She admitted **have seen / to having seen / to see / to being seen** him on several occasions.

(8) They are the sort of people who care about nothing except **get / to get / got / getting** ahead.

(9) No event, however minor, can occur in a small provincial town without **its being noticed / it being noticed / its noticing / it to be noticed**.

(10) How do you manage to make him **to cook / cooking / cooked / cook** your breakfast every day ?

score : ... × 10 = ◯

d) Même exercice.

(1) The stuntman was made **do / to do / doing / to be done** the car accident scene 3 times.

(2) She hadn't got round to **tell / have told / telling / being told** him about the dent in his car.

(3) She dreaded ... the children the dog had been run over by a truck and killed, but she decided there was no use ... around the bush. **(to tell-to beat / to telling-beating / telling-beating / having to tell-to beat)**

(4) Many children's cartoons and toys encourage them **to grow up thinking / growing up to think / to**

(1) **grow up to think / growing up to thinking** violence is normal.

(5) Did you see that man **to drive / drive / drove / having driven** through the red light ?

(6) After questioning him for 3 hours, the police superintendant got him **denounce / to denounce / denouncing / to be denounced** his accomplices.

(7) He had dreamed ... a famous rock star but he ended up ... the drums in a night-club. **(of being-in playing / to be-playing / of being-playing / being-playing)**

(8) How **get rid of / getting rid of / got rid of / to get rid of** nuclear waste is an issue that arouses may impassioned debates in industrialized countries.

(9) She realized she was about **to pick / to picking / pick / picking** a fight with her husband over nothing again but couldn't help herself.

(10) He got sent to the Principal's office **through hitting / to have hit / to hit / for hitting** another little boy.

(11) When somebody asks me why I believe in God, I really don't know what **answer / answering / to be answered / to answer**.

(12) Why did you leave your car engine **running / run / to run / be running** ?

(13) There's no **deny / denying / be denied / have denied** her children are extremely well-bred.

(14) It's such a complex situation that the only thing you can do is **wait and see / to wait and see / waiting and seeing / to waiting and seeing**.

(15) In his press conference the President went on **re-emphasize / to be re-emphasized / to re-emphasize**

INFINITIF ET GÉRONTIF

/ **re-emphasizing** the importance of forcing the pace of Western European integration.

(16) He gets me **believing / to believing / believe / to believe** that I can't do anything right and that everything is my fault.

(17) Why do you always try ... him ... guilty ? **(making-to feel / to make-to feel / to make-feel / to make-feeling)**

(18) She accompanied her back to her house and stayed there ... coffee and ... for 2 hours. **(drink-talk / drinking-talking / in drinking-talking / having drunk-having talked)**

(19) The house was so quiet that the water could be heard **to drip / drip / dripped / have dripped** in the sink at the other end of the hall.

(20) You can help save the Earth ... candy wrappers in a waste-basket instead of on the sidewalk and ... showers to under 15 minutes. **(while throwing-limiting / throwing-limiting / on throwing-limiting / by throwing-limiting)**

score : ... × 5 = ◯

e) Réécrivez les phrases en utilisant les amorces proposées.

(1) His idea is to go mountaineering in New Zealand.
He plans ...

(2) You mustn't answer your mother back.
I can't stand ...

INFINITIF ET GÉRONTIF

(3) Tom Thumb eventually succeeded in finding his way home.
He eventually managed ...

(4) I no longer read novels, they bore me to tears.
I've given up ...

(5) It would be a bad thing if I lost money in that deal.
I can't afford ...

(6) You can invite your friends for the weekend ; I don't object to it.
I don't mind ...

(7) Suppose we took the children to the circus.
What about ...

(8) Mother wants us to go to the dentist twice a year.
Mother insists on ...

(9) I'm sure this young soprano will be a great success.
She is certain ...

(10) "You neglect all your duties", she said to him.
She accused him ...

score : ... × 10 = ◯

f) Complétez le texte en mettant les verbes en italiques à la forme qui convient : infinitif, avec ou sans to, ou gérondif.

On (1) *to come to grips* with Japanese economic imperialism.

There's no (2) *to deny* the Rockefeller Center deal was an unsettling reminder of the decline of US financial dominance and Japan's simultaneous rise. Americans resent

INFINITIF ET GÉRONTIF

Japan's **(3)** *to become* a competitive industrial country. They are sick of **(4)** *to hear* how great Japan is and how rotten the US is. All the more so as the media focus on the negative aspects of America while **(5)** *to downplay* societal problems in Japan. If the press keeps **(6)** *to report* that the US is declining, people will believe it and it is likely **(7)** *to become* a self-fulfilling prophecy.

Japan is bound **(8)** *to provoke* jealousy and **(9)** *to perceive* as an imagined threat to the west. There's no doubt Japan is a great place **(10)** *to live* and **(11)** *to do* business in. Americans are constantly made **(12)** *to remember* Japan's product quality, work habits and economic power. But less often is it charged with **(13)** *to be* a leader in over-fishing, destruction of rain forests and exploitation of endangered and protected species. One reason cited by the Japanese for **(14)** *not to buy* American products is poor quality. What then explains their resistance to **(15)** *to buy* American rice, beef, oranges... ? It's high time Americans realized that the Japanese would rather **(16)** *to buy* Japanese products. There's nothing wrong with that just as there is nothing wrong with Americans **(17)** *to want* **(18)** *to buy* American products. The problem of America then is : how **(19)** *to retain* its role as a world leader or else how **(20)** *to get used to* **(21)** *to see* the Japanese **(22)** *to take* their place.

Many Americans would like their government **(23)** *to impose* higher tariffs on Japanese imports. But hadn't the US better **(24)** *to double* its efforts **(25)** *to become* more competitive ?

score : ... × 4 = ◯

58 INFINITIF ET GÉRONDIF

g) Traduisez ces phrases.

(1) En entrant dans la cuisine j'ai senti une odeur de gaz.
(2) Il n'y a pas moyen de faire démarrer ma voiture, inutile de noyer le moteur.
(3) Autrefois les parents pouvaient punir leurs enfants en les enfermant dans leur chambre.
(4) Lave-toi les mains avant de passer à table.
(5) J'attends de vos nouvelles avec impatience.
(6) Beaucoup de gens se sentent plus en sécurité en portant une arme sur eux.
(7) Elle s'est brûlée en sortant le poulet du four.
(8) Personne ne peut s'habituer à être l'objet de discrimination.
(9) Il a réussi à vaincre la peur qu'il avait de plonger.
(10) On m'a découragé, étant enfant, d'écrire de la poésie.

score : ... × 10 =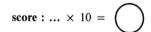

9. LE PRÉSENT

a) **Complétez les phrases en mettant les verbes en italiques au présent simple ou au présent progressif.**

(1) There's no understanding what she *talk about*.
(2) He always *demand* meat for dinner.
(3) Corn *grow* in warm, humid conditions.
(4) Knitting *require* a lot of patience.
(5) Tomorrow night they *show Gone with the Wind* on TV again.
(6) "How *you - feel* today ?" "Not too bad, but I (7) *not - feel* like doing anything."
(8) Who *sit* next to your brother in the stands over there ?
(9) What *we - do* next ?
(10) Look at him ! He *stuff* himself with a big banana split.
(11) He usually never *touch* ice-cream.
(12) Heineken beer-mats *bear* Van Gogh's self-portrait.
(13) She *iron* the shirt you (14) *look for*.
(15) People *start* to realize that flying (16) *become* more and more dangerous.
(17) Whenever I *take* a nap in the afternoon, I (18) *wake up* with a headache.
(19) I *forever - forget* this announcer's name.
(20) The exception *prove* the rule.
(21) The President *come back* from his West Indies trip tomorrow night.
(22) Why *you - be* so critical about it all of a sudden ?

LE PRÉSENT

(23) I asked you to stop biting your nails, *you - hear* me ? But you (24) *not - listen* again !

(25) When we *go* abroad next summer, we intend to do a lot of sightseeing.

score : ... × 4 = ◯

b) Même exercice.

(1) Every year, people *donate* money to Unicef.
(2) Look at this headline : ''After an 18-month separation hostages *meet* their families. ''
(3) Stop that noise, you *get* on my nerves.
(4) The United Nations *try* to find a solution to world hunger now.
(5) Before he *go* to bed at night, he (6) *eat* a bed-time snack.
(7) With the fall of the Berlin wall, we *see* history in the making.
(8) More and more people *die* of lung cancer every year.
(9) They *spend* their Christmas holiday in the Caribbean this year.
(10) I *see* double at the moment.
(11) Give her my love when you *see* her.
(12) As soon as my head *touch* the pillow I (13) *fall* asleep.
(14) Their aunt *expect* to see them for her 80th birthday-party.
(15) *You-think* of a solution to my problem ?

- **(16)** He *think* her children **(17)** *lack* in affection.
- **(18)** Now the defendant *stand up* and **(19)** *walk* to the witness-box.
- **(20)** "Please, Di, don't... you *be* stupid" said Prince Charles to the camera-shy Princess.
- **(21)** Poor thing ! She *have* a nervous breakdown.
- **(22)** We usually *have* dinner somewhat later but this evening we **(23)** *take* the children to the circus.
- **(24)** Look at them ! They *really-look* for trouble.
- **(25)** I *look* forward to hearing from you.

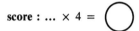

score : ... × 4 =

10. LES TEMPS DU PASSÉ

a) Complétez en mettant les verbes en italiques au prétérit simple ou au prétérit progressif. Attention à la place des adverbes.

They had flown to Dallas in the morning and now
(1) *to await* their connecting flight to Boston.
He told me he **(2)** *to change* jobs soon.
It **(3)** *to take* them 3 hours to drive to Belfast.
When the bomb **(4)** *to blow* his hospital apart, the doctor **(5)** *to tend* patients on the far side of town.
Lying on the grass, she looked at the sky where larks **(6)** *to fly* around.
When the plane **(7)** *to crash* over the Alps, it **(8)** *to snow* heavily.
He's a lonely man. His wife **(9)** *to pass away* last autumn.
She **(10)** *to check out* of the hotel at 11 o'clock.
"You **(11)** *not to wake me up*." "I **(12)** *to read*."
Three hours after the newlyweds had left, the guests **(13)** *still to dance*.
At one time his uncle **(14)** *to own* a racing stable.
Walking back to his hotel, he **(15)** *to pass by* the tennis courts where a tournament for juniors **(16)** *to play*.
What on earth **(17)** *you/ to do* in the bathroom at 3 AM with your ski-shoes on ?
He **(18)** *to work* on his battery, when, suddenly, he

(19) *to notice* he (20) *to watch* by a group of young children.

score : ... × 5 = ◯

b) Complétez en mettant les verbes en italiques au prétérit ou au present perfect, simple ou progressif.

I can't put a name on this man's face, but I (1) *to see* him before.
Scientific advancement during the last 20 years (2) *to give* us a new way of life.
As I didn't have any money when I was a student, I (3) *to have to* work my way through college.
This cave is unsafe, even the bats (4) *to leave* it.
Millions of people (5) *to be unemployed* during the Great Depression.
Do you know that Shakespeare (6) *to write* sonnets ?
Stop that ! You (7) *to go* too far.
During his furlough the captain (8) *to call on* his nephews in Liverpool.
J. Updike (9) *to be born* in Pennsylvania and (10) *to be educated* at Harvard. He (11) *to publish* many books, among them *the Centaur*, a novel.
English (12) *to replace* French as the language of diplomacy.
While in Washington, we (13) *to visit* the Lincoln Memorial.
You're late, it's half past eight. Where (14) *you/ go to* all day ?

Last month I **(15)** *to visit* the Eiffel Tower but I **(16)** *not/ can* see anything because there **(17)** *to be* a heavy fog.

She **(18)** *to lose* her keys. She **(19)** *to look for* them for 20 minutes but she **(20)** *not/ to find* them yet.

score : ... × 5 = ◯

c) Même exercice.

The weather **(1)** *to be* much cooler a week ago.

He **(2)** *to work* in a biscuit factory since he left his homeland.

This editor-in-chief **(3)** *to publish* American comics for the past 15 years.

Since the Afghan war the carpet trade **(4)** *severely to curtail*.

One of the features of our city park is an avenue of redwood trees that **(5)** *to import* from California a hundred years ago.

Haroun Tazieff **(6)** *to be interested in* volcanoes and earthquakes for over 40 years.

In August 1963 Martin Luther King **(7)** *to lead* the Civil Rights demonstration and **(8)** *to make* his famous speech "I have a dream".

I **(9)** *to wait* for my call to be put through for 15 minutes.

Since the first Earth Day in 1970, environmentalism **(10)** *to mushroom* into a diverse and imaginative movement.

score : ... × 10 = ◯

LES TEMPS DU PASSÉ

d) Complétez les phrases en ajoutant for, since ou ago aux expressions en italiques.

(1) The lawn has not been mown *3 weeks*.
(2) *A week* some clumsy and dishonest person backed into my fender and then drove off without leaving a note.
(3) How many people have been killed by car bombs in Ireland *1971* ?
(4) The heatwave started *10 days*.
(5) He is a careless driver but he hasn't had an accident *he bought his Austin*.
(6) It seems to me this highway has been under repair *ages*.
(7) *2 months* a man lost his life while sky-diving.
(8) They haven't had a Christmas tree in the house *the children left*.
(9) Their Friday night poker game was a tradition that had been going on *years*.
(10) *He stopped smoking* he's put on 12 pounds.

score : ... × 10 = ◯

e) Remettez les éléments en ordre de façon à reconstituer une phrase cohérente.

(1) been / Broadway / his / for / on / two / has / years / play
(2) married / about / complaining / ever / he / bills / been / run / since / she / her / up / has / he / the / has

66 LES TEMPS DU PASSÉ

  (3) has / written / to / the / moved / are / he / has / abroad / excellent / he / since / books / be / supposed
  (4) the / since / Indies / last / three / blew / over / tornado / the / is / West / it / years
  (5) bungee-jumping / two / known / as / recently / to / except / a / sky-divers / as / or / mountain-climbers / ago / was / few / little / years

score : ... × 20 = ◯

f) Trouver dans la colonne B les phrases qui ont un lien logique avec celles de la colonne A.

A

  (1) How long is it since
  (2) How long
  (3) How long has
  (4) How long ago
  (5) Since when

B

  (a) were you a travelling salesman ?
  (b) has slavery been abolished ?
  (c) you asked the bell-boy to bring up your breakfast ?
  (d) were women given the right to vote ?
  (e) his secretary been working with him ?

score : ... × 20 = ◯

LES TEMPS DU PASSÉ 67

g) Choisissez la solution qui convient.

(1) Ever since his son **is born / has been born / had been born / was born** he has worked at building up his business for him.

(2) How long **are you writing / do you write / have you been writing / had it been written** dramatic criticism for this review ?

(3) He feels a deep affection for his friend's son whom he **had known / knew / was knowing / has known** since he was 4.

(4) She was furious at her aunt who left her no money. She **had nursed / nursed / would have nursed / was nursing** the old lady for 6 months.

(5) Only 4 weeks ago, he **was turned down / turned down / has been turning down / has turned** a request from his manager to move up a crucial meeting from December to January.

(6) All of a sudden he remembered that yesterday he **had promised / promised / was promising / had been promising** he would call her.

(7) The RSPCA and other groups ... for years to change the law on animal experiments, but so far their campaigns ... with no success. **(have tried-met / have tried-have met / tried-have met / were trying-has been met)**

(8) She cannot meet expenses on the money she makes. She hasn't bought a new dress **since / last / in / this** months.

(9) **Since when / How long is it since / How long has it been since / How long** did he work as a chef in this Tottenham restaurant ?

(10) It was a long time since anyone **dared / had dared**

/ **has dared** / **was daring** mention her name to me.
(11) The article I wrote **a week since** / **a week ago** / **for a week** / **ever since** was turned down by a dozen magazines.
(12) The judge was wondering why the jury **had deliberated** / **has deliberated** / **deliberated** / **has been deliberating** so long the day before.
(13) How long ago **was Ellis Island turned into** / **did Ellis Island turn into** / **has Ellis Island turned into** / **has Ellis Island been turning into** a museum ?
(14) Tourism in Israel has been on a steady downward slide since the Palestinian uprising **has begun** / **is beginning** / **begins** / **began** a year ago.
(15) The little house they **buy** / **are buying** / **bought** / **have had to buy** was similar to the one they had rented years ago just after their marriage.
(16) **How long ago** / **How long is it since** / **When** / **Since when** has Washington been the capital of the United States ?
(17) It's about time you **had started** / **started** / **have started** / **was starting** looking for another job.
(18) In the last couple of years, her affection for him **was helping** / **helped** / **has helped** / **is helping** him to get through some of the darkest moments of his life.
(19) He **did find** / **was finding** / **has been finding** / **founded** the note-book, which he thought he had lost weeks ago, in the top drawer of his desk.
(20) Over the past decade environmental activism **is gaining** / **has gained** / **gained** / **will have gained** momentum.
(21) She really loved that patchwork spread **quilting 50 years ago** / **quilted 50 years ago** / **quilted in 50**

LES TEMPS DU PASSÉ

years / **being quilted 50 years ago** by her grandmother.

(22) Since a week ago he **became / had become / was becoming / has become** a hero with his photograph in every paper in America.

(23) While on vacation in the south of France he **has rented / was renting / rented / has been renting** a villa near Cannes.

(24) Very little ... in this village since I first ... it 30 years ago. **(has changed-visited / has changed-have visited / changed-had visited / has changed-have visited)**

(25) How long **is it since / was it since / had it been since / is it going to be since** they set up their new branch in San Francisco ?

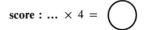

score : ... × 4 =

11. LE FUTUR

Complétez avec une des solutions proposées. Une de ces phrases comporte 4 solutions justes.

(1) The day I leave the army **is / would be / will be / has been** the happiest in my life.

(2) "There's been an accident down the road, ... an ambulance". "Call the fire brigade instead." "... that." **(I'm calling-I'm going to / I'm going to call-I do / I'm going to call-I'll do / I will be calling-I'm going to do)**

(3) When **are you moving / do you move / will you be moving / are you to move** to your new apartment ?

(4) I'd better get home, the children **have wondered / will be wondering / shall be wondering / wonder** what has happened to me.

(5) The situation is bad enough but I think the worse **was yet bound to come / is yet to come / was yet to come / will yet come**.

(6) He **will / is going to / was to / was about to** abandon all hope of being rescued when he heard the rescue dogs yapping in the distance.

(7) I am sure her play **is to be / is going to be / is being / is bound to be** a great success.

(8) Ask no questions and you **shall be / are / will be / are going to** told no lies.

LE FUTUR

(9) Next month we ... to rent a boat and cruise on the canals. It ... great ! **(are planning-is going to be / are planning-is about to be / plan-will / are going to plan-is going to be).**

(10) The shopkeeper said that from now on they **wouldn't open / wouldn't have opened / will have opened / will open** until 2:30 PM.

(11) Of course I'll ask him when he **would pay / paid / will pay / will have paid** me back.

(12) Tomorrow the Queen **is about to leave / is yet to leave / shall leave / leaves** for Balmoral for a family weekend.

(13) I **am to continue / shall continue / am continuing / will have continued** to consider him a friend whatever happens.

(14) The hundreds of petty drug-dealers that swarm the ill-famed streets of big cities **are being / would be / shall have been / are bound to be** apprehended one day.

(15) In a few years, Hong Kong, the British crown colony **reverts / shall revert / is about to revert / will revert** to the mainland's control.

(16) She explained to me that the doctor had told her that she **expected / had expected / was expecting / will expect** twins.

(17) The secretary couldn't tell him where the meeting **was to take / is to take / will take / is going to take** place.

(18) You'll feel less nervous after you **will sleep / have slept / will have slept / sleep** for a little while.

(19) By this time tomorrow I hope an agreement **will have reached / will have been reached / will be reached / will reach** between the two companies.

(20) He **is to have been / is to be / will have been / was to have been** operated on, but his bad physical condition made this impossible.

(21) When I **will marry / shall marry / marry / will be married** I want a wife who can cook.

(22) By evening the rain **will be turning / is about to turn / is turning / has turned** to showers.

(23) Present statistics indicate that the average Briton who reaches the age of 65 **was to spend / will have spent / shall be spending / would spend** nine years of his life watching TV.

(24) As soon as the pilot **is going to receive / will receive / receives / will have received** the come-in signal, he will circle the field in preparation for landing.

(25) The day will come when sophisticated computers **are / are going to / are being / will be** within the reach of the ordinary man.

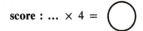

12. LE CONDITIONNEL

a) Complétez par should ou would à la forme (affirmative ou négative) qui convient.

(1) Mr Peters is not in. ... you like to leave a message ?
(2) What ... you do with all that money if you won the lottery ?
(3) Everybody ... be willing to defend their principles.
(4) I ... feel much safer if you walked me home.
(5) ... you be getting ready to leave ?
(6) Why ... he go looking for birds if he feels like it.
(7) If you can, you ... take a walk every day.
(8) I ... love to stay for dinner but (9) I ... want to impose on you.
(10) People ... always vote on election day.
(11) You ... be upset with her. She didn't really mean what she said.
(12) ... you pass me the butter please ?
(13) What I am telling you ... get out.
(14) What ... you like to do tonight ?
(15) It's almost eleven. The children ... be asleep by now.
(16) I ... enjoy working part-time. (17) It ... be a distraction and I need distraction.
(18) ... you mind carrying these bags for me please ?
(19) Children ... obey their parents without question but

74 LE CONDITIONNEL

(20) parents ... never hit a child.

score : ... × 5 = ◯

b) Complétez les phrases en mettant les verbes en italiques au conditionnel présent ou au conditionnel passé : would **ou** would have + participe passé.

(1) If they had listened to Inspector Murray, they *to catch* the thieves red-handed.
(2) If her husband became more famous, she *to see* less of him.
(3) He's got a good job and a decent salary, what more *he / can / to want* ?
(4) With the excitement of her son's homecoming she probably *not / to finish* cooking dinner on time.
(5) When the Vietnam war broke out, he *not / to consider* dodging the draft.
(6) *You / to be interested in* doing some library research work for a sociology professor ?
(7) You *never / to notice* if it hadn't been for me.
(8) She *not / to want* her ex-husband back in the house now after all these months.
(9) If you hadn't been speeding, the police *not / to arrest* you.
(10) Andrew stood me up again. I *never / to expect* it of him.

score : ... × 10 = ◯

LE CONDITIONNEL 75

c) Complétez avec une des solution proposées. Une de ces phrases comporte 4 solutions justes.

(1) She felt so wretched that if she had been alone she **would burst / would have burst / would be bursting / will have burst** into tears.
(2) Since you don't go in much for crowded resorts, the best thing for you **was / would be / would have been / are** to go to the Auvergne.
(3) Here is a pocket-knife I brought along. I thought you **need / might have needed / might need / may need** it if you go camping.
(4) He realized that in order to get past him, he **should have to / will have to / will have had to / would have to** use force, perhaps even violence.
(5) Make up your mind ; which puppet show **had you / would you / did you / should you** prefer to go to ?
(6) She felt sure they **left / will leave / would have left / will have left** by ten o'clock.
(7) What a pity your brother wasn't able to come to England with you, he **would have been able to / would be able to / was able to / will be able to** help you.
(8) Reagan is quoted as saying : "There were a number of times when I thought : **can you do / will you be able / will you do / could you do** that job if you hadn't been an actor ?"
(9) If you love somebody you often **would want / want / wanted / shall want** to have children with them.
(10) If you **would need / had needed / will need / should need** anything, feel free to ask.
(11) The promoters had intended to build a big hotel

LE CONDITIONNEL

overlooking the river ; it **would be / will have been / would have been / should be** the most luxurious in the area.

(12) Is there anything I **could do / would do / would be able to do / was able to do** for you ?

(13) If you **lived / would live / live / had lived** in Paris you have to get used to parking problems.

(14) If you **should have / would / should / will** hear a strange noise in the middle of the night, call the police.

(15) If you **will come / come / had come / would come** to this small town you would make a good living as a vet.

(16) She **might as well have waited / may as well have waited / could as well have waited / might as well wait** until next week to do her spring cleaning.

(17) He **shouldn't possibly have done / shouldn't possibly do / will not possibly have done / couldn't possibly have done** that to her.

(18) If one **had / has / would have / should have** good health, one should feel fortunate.

(19) If you **wouldn't / shouldn't / hadn't / won't** give up smoking altogether, at least buy low-tar cigarettes.

(20) Suppose you **would forget / should forget / should have forgotten / will forget** to register, you wouldn't be able to vote in the June election.

score : ... × 5 = ◯

13. LES AUXILIAIRES MODAUX

A. FORMES SIMPLES

a) Complétez les phrases avec l'un des auxiliaires modaux suivants :

   (i) mustn't - can - could - may - should

(1) You ... ask Mary, but I doubt whether she'll lend you a penny.
(2) One ... always get up from a meal feeling one (3) ... eat a little more.
(4) We ... judge everyone by our own standards.
(5) She's very gifted. She ... mimic just about anyone.

   (ii) might - could - can't - needn't - must

(6) "What does that sign say ?" "I don't know, I ... see from here".
(7) You ... worry any more. You've just won a full scholarship to Stanford University.
(8) "What about eating out tonight ?" "That's a good idea, we ... have Mexican food for a change".

- **(9)** I ... remember to pick up some groceries at the shop on my way home.
- **(10)** You never know. You ... run into them at the Derby.

score : ... × 10 = ◯

b) Complétez les phrases avec will, shall, should **ou** would.

- **(1)** Many people think violent scenes... be censored on TV.
- **(2)** ... I make you another drink ?
- **(3)** We'll have supper in 30 minutes. Everybody ... be home by then.
- **(4)** I keep telling him to fasten his seat-belt, but he ...
- **(5)** ... you help me serve those drinks, please ?
- **(6)** If you feel flat and tired at the end of the day, you ... come with me to my aerobics classes.
- **(7)** An American naturalist says that plants, like human beings, ... faint or pass out if they are very "distressed".
- **(8)** Who... I say called ?
- **(9)** ... you like me to water your plants while you're away ?
- **(10)** She has a grand piano ? She ..., she is so musical.

score : ... × 10 = ◯

B. FORMES COMPOSÉES ET ÉQUIVALENTS

a) Choisissez la solution qui convient.

(1) In the 1960s Josephine Baker **wouldn't be allowed / would not have allowed / wouldn't have been able / wouldn't have been allowed** in the restaurant which now bears her name.

(2) They **should never resort / can never resort / should never have resorted / ought never to resort** to violence when they lived together.

(3) You **ought not to / should not have / may have / ought not to have** take professional reverses so hard !

(4) He always told me that when he had a project in mind, he **may have / had to / will / shall** finish it.

(5) No family **should allow to / should be allowed to / ought to allow / shouldn't be allowed to** have more than six children nowadays !

(6) The doctor told him to give up alcohol and cigarettes, but he **shouldn't / mustn't / wouldn't / would**.

(7) It **ought to be / must be / could be / must have been** hard on the children when their mother died.

(8) Many people believe that live animals **shouldn't be used / wouldn't be used / shouldn't use / ought not to use** for medical experiments.

(9) He made her bring out sandwiches for all of us so we **wouldn't have to / hadn't to / didn't have / will not have to** stop working for lunch.

(10) She graduated from a good university. She **must be / can't be / can be / could be** all that stupid.

(11) She didn't seem to be aware that her friends **can be / mustn't have been / might have been / may be** shocked by her attitude.

(12) Millions of people have poor eyesight that ... corrected with glasses. They ... read the title of a book but not the book. **(can't be-could have / mustn't be-might be able to / couldn't-were able to / can't be-might be able to)**.

(13) You **must / ought not / didn't need / needn't** be frightened. I chained the dog.

(14) Do you think he **was able to / will be able to / may have / was allowed to** do anything for us when we come to Paris ?

(15) She is 45 now ; 20 years ago she **can't be / must be / must have been / ought to be** a pretty woman.

(16) What's the good of belonging to a trade union if you **shouldn't / wouldn't / won't / shan't** stand up by your principles.

(17) She **can't have lost / mustn't lose / mustn't have lost / can't lose** her engagement ring. It was here a minute ago.

(18) I keep telling them that they **ought / shall / will / would** make the same mistakes over and over again.

(19) In some hospitals patients ... wait for months to be admitted. Some operating-rooms ... because of cuts in government funding. **(may-have had to close / may-had had to close / would be-have had to close / might-had had to be closed)**.

(20) **May people / Might people / Should people allow / Should people be allowed** to do their own policing ?

LES AUXILIAIRES MODAUX

Attention dans les 5 dernières phrases c'est la solution qui ne convient pas qu'il faut trouver.

(21) She's never had any children but she **could have adopted** / **would have adopted** / **may have adopted** / **might have adopted** some.

(22) You **don't have to** / **needn't** / **haven't to** / **shouldn't** be ashamed of yourself for wanting to be rich.

(23) Remind him that he **might not** / **mustn't** / **shouldn't** / **can't** smoke in this restaurant.

(24) After they got married they both **had to** / **were obliged to** / **could have** / **were compelled to** work to make ends meet.

(25) You **must** / **ought** / **should** / **had better** be more conciliatory if you want to come to an agreement with your friend.

score : ... × 4 = ◯

b) Reformulez ces phrases en utilisant un auxiliaire modal et sans en modifier le sens.

(1) He's a student and he's got a flat of his own. I suppose his parents helped him.

(2) Lots of women today don't know how to cook.

(3) Why don't you try that cheap hotel down the street ; there's a slight chance that they'll take you in.

(4) I'm sure he didn't buy a Japanese car, he doesn't like them.

(5) The best thing for you to do would be to reserve your seats if you want to see that show.

LES AUXILIAIRES MODAUX

(6) You aren't obliged to hoover the floor every day, you know !
(7) They were obliged to remodel their house but they couldn't get a loan from the bank.
(8) Perhaps your flat will be burgled while you are away.
(9) I'm telling you this, but don't let it go any further.
(10) It's essential that you carry traveler's checks if you travel extensively.

score : ... × 10 = ◯

c) A l'aide des amorces, reformulez ces phrases sans en modifier le sens, en utilisant les équivalents des auxiliaires modaux en italiques.

(1) You *may not* take your dog on the train with you.
When she took the train to Eton, she ...
(2) When you *can* drive a car in America, it's a mark of being an adult.
... to drive a car ...
(3) I'm sorry but I *must* tell you that you are not eligible for this scholarship.
I'm sorry to ...
(4) "You *needn't* drink your cocktail if you don't like it."
She assured me ...
(5) I'd *prefer* to park in a car-park than on this deserted street.
I' ...
(6) He outlived his wife by 10 years ; *it was his destiny*.
He ...

(7) She *couldn't* make him understand her point of view.
She still ...
(8) You *needn't* look up her number because I've got it in my address-book. Here it is.
I saved time, I...
(9) It *would be better* for you not to flaunt your wealth.
You ...
(10) He *is not likely* to be a terrorist.
He ...

score : ... × 10 = ◯

C. TESTS RÉCAPITULATIFS

a) Choisissez la solution qui convient.

(1) He handed me the poems he had just written so that I **may / might / can / would** judge for myself.
(2) She never flies anywhere for fear the plane **would be hijacked / could be hijacked / should be hijacked / might be hijacked**.
(3) **Would / Should / Ought to / Will** the rash on your legs become more extensive, call a doctor.
(4) As awful as it **may / can / should / shall** sound, racism appears to be part of human nature.
(5) I see no reason why women **shouldn't be / wouldn't be / may not be / won't be** professionally ambitious.
(6) It's totally unacceptable that Britain's universities **could / should / would / may** remain bastions of male power and privilege.

(7) Whatever the price **may be** / **could be** / **should be** / **ought to be** I'll take a trip around the world.

(8) Her husband was furious that she **might** / **may** / **should** / **would** want to go out to see a film on his first evening home after a week.

(9) How I wish **to get over** / **I should get over** / **I could get over** / **I had got over** this cold. I've had it for a week now.

(10) After what had happened between them, he certainly didn't expect that **she should call** / **she will call** / **she may call** / **her to call** him.

score : ... × 10 = ◯

b) Traduisez en évitant le mot à mot.

(1) Ils ne devraient pas tarder.
(2) Elle a dû oublier de mettre du sel.
(3) Tout le monde doit mourir !
(4) Vous auriez dû mettre votre adresse au dos de l'enveloppe.
(5) Dois-je vous faire un paquet, Madame ?
(6) Il a 18 ans. Il doit prendre sa première leçon de conduite demain.
(7) Il s'est fait tout seul. Il ne doit rien à ses parents.
(8) On ne doit pas battre un enfant.
(9) De nombreux accidents sont dus à des automobilistes conduisant en état d'ébriété.
(10) Il devait se couper avec ce couteau, ça c'était sûr !

score : ... × 10 = ◯

14. LES VERBES COMPOSÉS

a) Conjuguez les verbes en italiques en veillant à la place de la particule. Il peut y avoir plusieurs possibilités.

(1) Can you *look up* her telephone number in the phone book please ?
(2) Under no circumstances should a spy *give away* any information.
(3) He is a late sleeper ; there's no *wake up* him before midday.
(4) If things get worse, we'll have to *close down* two of our branches.
(5) Has the store delivered your new stove ? You should *call up* them.
(6) He grew sideburns, but soon didn't like them. So he *shave off* them.
(7) He's just *run across* a friend of his at the bank.
(8) She's been missing from school for a week. I might *drop in* on her this afternoon.
(9) We must *work out* something to help him.
(10) Do you think we'll ever *run out* of oil ?

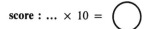

score : ... × 10 =

86 LES VERBES COMPOSÉS

b) Remplacez le verbe en italiques par un verbe à particule de même sens, en choisissant une des particules de la liste suivante.

off - on - out - into - up - away

(1) He hired two private detectives *to investigate* the burglary of his jewellery store. (to look)
(2) Why did you *stop* learning Japanese ? (to give)
(3) I'll probably *visit* you tomorrow. (to call)
(4) Did you *discover* who left that message on your answering machine ? (to find)
(5) Be careful when you *leave* the bus. (to get)
(6) The excuse you *invented* was not very convincing. (to make)
(7) In this residential area five houses *were burgled* last summer. (to break)
(8) Soak your blouse in lukewarm water and the stain will *disappear*. (to wash)
(9) They *raised* their son to be a doctor but he dropped out of high school. (to bring)
(10) Most doctors *consider* alcoholism a disease, not a mark of immorality. (to look)

score : ... × 10 = ◯

c) Remplacez le verbe en italiques par un verbe à particule de même sens, choisi dans la liste suivante.

to fall for - to get something over with - to wait on - to stand for - to go on - to run into - to take after - to make out - to live through - to take over.

(1) I can't *understand* why he insisted on enlisting before call-up.

(2) I won't *tolerate* such bad language.

(3) It's high time you *finished* your doctorate dissertation.

(4) Who would *replace* the president in case he should die unexpectedly ?

(5) The moment I set my eyes on those antique fire-dogs at the flea market I *loved* them.

(6) He *met* his ex-wife *unexpectedly* as he was strolling in the foyer of the Opera House during the interval.

(7) Are you being *served*, Madam ?

(8) What's *happening* here ?

(9) She *resembles* her grand-mother on her father's side.

(10) He served a year in Vietnam and was lucky enough to *survive* it.

score : ... × 10 = $\bigcirc$

1) Choisissez l'équivalent du verbe en italiques.

(1) She shouldn't have *turned down* their offer.
(**accepted / overlooked / scorned / refused**)

(2) When she turned the ignition key, the engine

started roaring and then *died out*. **(stalled / spluttered / purred / hummed)**

(3) Mother knows I skipped the history class last week ; my brother must have *told on* me. **(informed on / spied on / prevented / incited)**

(4) I didn't think he would *take up* with such a girl. **(resent / take out / become involved / denigrate)**

(5) If she were *to back out* now, it would only prove her cowardice. **(to turn back / to decide not to do it / to persist / to proceed)**

(6) It was *given out* that the President's daughter was going to divorce her third husband. **(refuted / kept secret / underplayed / announced)**

(7) I resent being told *to hang up* quickly whenever I am on the phone. **(to lift the receiver / to hold on / to put the receiver back on the hook / to wait)**

(8) A spendthrift is a person who doesn't *put* money *away* for the proverbial "rainy day". **(invest / save / give away / make profitable)**

(9) Children of mixed parentage are likely *to run up* against difficulties. **(to encounter / to fight / to avoid / to be unaware of)**

(10) They decided *to cut down on* their drinking to weekends only. **(to stop / to diversify / to indulge in / to reduce)**.

score : ... × 10 =

LES VERBES COMPOSÉS   89

e) Complétez avec la particule qui convient.

(1) We waited a long time but nobody showed **up / on / in / Ø**.

(2) He's a reckless driver, but he hasn't run **on / into / over / onto** anybody yet !

(3) He was mugged in the street, but managed to knock the man **up / in / about / out**.

(4) She can spend hours at the airport watching planes taking **away / out / of / off**.

(5) He pointed **out / in / on / Ø** to her that he had always left it to her to supervise the children in everyday matters.

(6) Hold **out / on / in / onto** a moment, Sir, I'll connect you to the Engineering Department.

(7) Don't walk so fast, I can't keep **along with / on with / up with / with** you.

(8) How does she get **along / onto / in / Ø** with her teenage children ?

(9) How much longer will I have to put **on with / along with / in / up with** the noise of that drill ?

(10) Being both frail and conscientious, she would wear herself **off / away / out / over** if she took that job.

score : ... × 10 = ◯

f) Répondez aux questions suivantes.

(1) Marilyn always switches off the lights when she leaves the house. Carol always switches on the lights.
Who is trying to save energy ?

LES VERBES COMPOSÉS

(2) Emily put on her nightgown and went to bed.
Erica put away her nightgown.
Who wears a nightgown to bed ?

(3) Sally looks down on her husband. Martha looks after her husband.
Who's the more devoted wife ?

(4) Larry came down with bronchitis. Bob came through bronchitis.
Who has recovered ?

(5) Nancy called for Dr. Williamson at 5 PM.
Christine called on Dr. Williamson at 5 PM.
Who went to Dr. Williamson's ?

(6) Sam stood in for me for the second time this week. George stood me up for the second time this week.
Who's the more reliable of my two friends ?

(7) Rose turns Frank on. Monica turns Frank off.
Whom is Frank likely to take to the restaurant ?

(8) My boss took to my friend Wendy. My boss took on my friend Dora.
Which girl got herself a job ?

(9) The union leader wants to call for a meeting. The manager wants to call off the meeting.
Who actually wants to find a solution to the problems of the company ?

(10) Joe set himself up as a millionaire. Harry set on the millionaire.
Who was more aggressive ?

score : ... × 10 = ◯

15. LES REPRISES VERBALES

A. LES "QUESTION-TAGS"

a) Ajoutez le « question-tag » qui convient.

(1) The president will talk on TV tonight, ... ?
(2) You've never heard that concerto, ... ?
(3) They're to be married in June, ... ?
(4) He couldn't have managed alone, ... ?
(5) You must take off your shoes before entering a mosque, ... ?
(6) He wouldn't steal that money, ... ?
(7) Evelyn really looks good today, ... ?
(8) She can't be that old, ... ?
(9) There was no bridge over that river, ... ?
(10) Prices went up again last month, ... ?

score : ... × 10 = $\bigcirc$

b) Choisissez le « tag » qui convient.

(1) She had to send for the doctor, **hadn't she ?** / **didn't she ?** / **did she ?**

(2) Let's go fishing on Sunday, **shall we ?** / will we ? / won't we ?

(3) He'd rather not tell her the bad news, **wouldn't he ?** / would he ? / had he ?

(4) You needn't lock the door, **need you ?** / don't you ? / do you ?

(5) That's good news, **isn't it ?** / is it ? / isn't that ?

(6) They should have thought about it before, **should they have ?** / should they ? / shouldn't they ?

(7) What he likes best is a good book, does he ? / isn't it ? / **is it ?**

(8) This food is hardly edible, **is it ?** / is this ? / isn't it ?

(9) Make sure this doesn't happen again, **won't you ?** / will you ? / don't you ?

(10) You'd never been mugged before, would you ? / **hadn't you ?** / had you ?

(11) It's been a very nice day today, is it ? / **hasn't it ?** / isn't it ?

(12) They had no right to do that, hadn't they ? / did they ? / **didn't they ?**

(13) Everybody came in on time, didn't one ? / didn't he ? / **didn't they ?**

(14) You and I are good friends, aren't you ? / **aren't we ?** / aren't they ?

(15) You've got your plane ticket with you, **haven't you ?** / don't you ? / have you ?

(16) There is nothing I can do for him, isn't there ? / is it ? / **is there ?**

(17) You said you didn't like horror films, **didn't you ?** / did you ? / don't you ?

(18) She never used to wear glasses, **didn't she ?** / did she ? / used she ?

LES REPRISES VERBALES

(19) Mind your own business, **will you ?** / **won't you ?** / **don't you ?**

(20) He had his hair cut yesterday, **hadn't he ?** / **had he ?** / **didn't he ?**

(21) I'm supposed to be there at six, **am I ?** / **aren't I ?** / **isn't it ?**

(22) Your luggage won't be too heavy, **will they ?** / **won't they ?** / **will it ?**

(23) She'd better keep her word, **hadn't she ?** / **wouldn't she ?** / **would she ?**

(24) No one knows why he took to the bottle, **don't they ?** / **does he ?** / **do they ?**

(25) He has to take his vitamins every day, **hasn't he ?** / **doesn't he ?** / **has he ?**

score : ... × 4 = ◯

B. LES « TAGS » DE RÉPONSE

a) Choisissez la reprise verbale qui convient.

(1) "The largest sumo wrestler in the world weighs 255 kilos." "He isn't ?" / "Does he ?" / "Is he ?" / "So does he."

(2) I don't think your father will ever forgive you for that, **but your mother will.** / **but your mother won't.** / **but your mother doesn't.** / **so will your mother.**

LES REPRISES VERBALES

(3) "That's Jean practising her scales again." "So it has." / "So she has." / "So it is." / "So that is."

(4) "I can't stand Coluche." "Oh, you can, can you ?" / "Can you ?" / "Neither can you." / "Oh, you can't, can't you ?"

(5) I don't think much of Woody Allen's humour, **but many people do.** / **so do many people.** / **but many people don't.** / **but many people don't think so.**

(6) He wasn't paying attention to me or **wasn't he ?** / **was he ?** / **he was.** / **he wasn't.**

(7) "Silicone Valley encourages people to be workaholics." "**So do Japanese firms.**" / "**Neither do Japanese firms.**" / "**Nor do Japanese firms.**" / "**But Japanese firms do.**"

(8) Her children live on hamburgers and coke, but **mine don't.** / **neither do mine.** / **mine don't either.** / **so they don't.**

(9) "He hasn't had breakfast yet." "**So has somebody else.**" / "**But somebody else hasn't.**" / "**Nobody else had.**" / "**Neither has anybody else.**"

(10) "Chinese cooking is said to be the best in the world." "**Neither is French cooking.**" / "**But French cooking is.**" / "**So is French cooking.**" / "**French cooking isn't either.**"

score : ... × 10 = 〇

b) Choisissez la reprise verbale qui convient.

(1) "Brian drops his h's." "**Of course lots of people don't.**" / "**Of course lots of people are.**" / "**So do lots of people.**" / "**Neither do lots of people**".

LES REPRISES VERBALES

(2) Spaniels and setters are good gundogs, **but German shepherds are.** / **neither are German shepherds.** / **but German shepherds do.** / **but German shepherds aren't.**

(3) "I don't believe in God or in any religion ; they are all lies." "Oh they are, are they ?" / "Oh they aren't, aren't they ?" / "Oh you do, do you ?" / "So you do".

(4) "Mozart died in extreme poverty." "So he didn't." / "So he did." / "So did he." / "So has he."

(5) I don't snore, **but my wife does.** / **doesn't my wife.** / **but my wife doesn't.** / **so does my wife.**

(6) I can hardly tell the difference, **so can I.** / **you can.** / **so can they.** / **neither can they.**

(7) Ants work very hard, **so do I.** / **neither do I.** / **so do they.** / **neither do they.**

(8) I'd rather work full time, **but lots of women would.** / **but lots of women wouldn't.** / **but lots of women had.** / **but lots of women hadn't.**

(9) « I saw the Loch Ness monster." "Did I ?" / "Didn't I ?" / "Did you ?" / "Didn't you ?"

(10) He never used to take a nap after lunch, **neither used his cats.** / **nor did his cats.** / **so did his cats.** / **so do his cats.**

score : ... × 10 = ◯

c) Parmi les quatre solutions proposées une seule est impossible. Cherchez l'intrus. Attention, dans une de ces phrases, il n'y a pas d'intrus.

(1) She says she must lose weight, **but she needn't.** / **but she doesn't have to.** / **but she must.** / **but she won't.**

(2) He didn't really mean what he said, **did he ?** / **"Didn't he ?"** / **"So he didn't."** / **"So he did."**

(3) I'm getting old but **everybody does.** / **so is everybody.** / **isn't everybody ?** / **everybody is.**

(4) Have another cup of tea, **will you ?** / **won't you ?** / **please do.** / **please have.**

(5) He believes in reincarnation, **doesn't he ?** / **"Does he ?"** / **"Oh, he does, does he ?"** / **"Oh, he doesn't ?"**

(6) They didn't expect him to be awarded the Nobel Prize, **and he wasn't.** / **so did I.** / **but he was.** / **neither did I.**

(7) He will probably not make a good husband, **nor will his brother.** / **his brother won't either.** / **but his brother won't.** / **neither will his brother.**

(8) "It's as well to be a man as a woman." **"Ha ! is it ?"** / **"It is, isn't it ?"** / **"Of course, it is."** / **"Of course, it isn't."**

(9) I don't think Paul would tell on me, **but Charles would.** / **but would Charles ?** / **but Charles wouldn't.** / **neither would Charles.**

(10) "Shall we stop and have a bite on the way ?" **"Yes, we shall."** / **"Yes, let's."** / **"Yes, let's do."** / **"Yes, let's stop."**

score : ... × 10 = ◯

16. LES QUESTIONS

a) Complétez les phrases avec un pronom interrogatif.

(1) ... won the Paris-Dakar race ? Vatanen.
(2) ... idea was it ? Not mine !
(3) ... is it to the fire-station ? 2 miles.
(4) ... did it take you to clean the mess in your room ? A half-hour.
(5) ... cars has he already wrecked ? Three.
(6) ... did you go out with last night ? William.
(7) ... one would you rather have ? The smaller one.
(8) ... is the Soviet flag ? Red.
(9) ... have you been all day ? At the library.
(10) ... was your flight delayed ? Because of the heavy fog.

score : ... × 10 = ◯

b) Posez les questions qui correspondent aux mots en italiques. Respectez le temps des verbes.

(1) He can get there *by bus*.
(2) The film "Gone with the Wind" is showing *next week*.
(3) The traffic was diverted *because of a roadblock*.

(4) *The English and the French* are building the Chunnel.
(5) This woman executive makes *$ 80,000* a year.
(6) Capital punishment was abolished *8 years ago* in France.
(7) There were lots of tourists *in Italy* last year.
(8) They'd like to go to Disneyland with *their children*.
(9) Queen Victoria ruled for *63 years*.
(10) He was arrested by *a plain-clothes policeman*.

score : ... × 10 =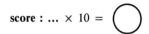

c) Même exercice.

(1) They left from *Victoria Station*.
(2) Her son takes after *his grand-father*.
(3) The policeman signalled him *to pull over*.
(4) *The criminals* were sent to the state prison.
(5) He should invite his *girl friend* to the theatre.
(6) I'd like to borrow a jack *to change my tyre*.
(7) He'd rather have voted for the *younger* congressman.
(8) *My neighbour's* car is parked on the wrong side of the street.
(9) They had to get up *at 6* to catch an early train.
(10) Her husband usually spends his holidays *fishing*.
(11) Mount Everest is *8,848 m*.
(12) They'll be spending the night at *uncle Frank's*.
(13) They used to spend Christmas *in the Bahamas*.
(14) I've already told you *once* to stop shouting.

(15) This has been going on *for ages*.
(16) You should feed the dog *twice a day*.
(17) There are about *30* million pets in Great Britain.
(18) We've been sunbathing *since 3 o'clock*.
(19) He apologized to his wife *for being late*.
(20) Our new apartment is *120 m²*, twice as big as the former one.

score : ... × 5 = ◯

d) Retrouvez les questions posées par un agent du service de l'immigration à Mr Hershfield à propos de son fils Sam.

(1) Sam Hershfield.
(2) H-E-R-S-H-F-I-E-L-D.
(3) 25.
(4) On June 2nd, in Hamburg, Germany.
(5) 132 Robbins Street, Brookline, Ma.
(6) Married.
(7) 6 feet.
(8) 169 lb.
(9) He's got big feet, size 9.
(10) He's tall, rather plain-looking as a matter of fact.

score : ... × 10 = ◯

100   LES QUESTIONS

e) Voici les réponses. Pour chacune d'elles proposez une question possible. Aidez-vous des mots en italiques lorsque cela est le cas.

(1) There's the news at 8 o'clock and then a soap opera.

(2) Ham and eggs and coffee with cream, *please waiter*.

(3) Cold and windy.

(4) There's roastbeef and Yorkshire pudding and strawberries for dessert.

(5) £ *30*, it's cheap for a tracksuit, but it was on sale.

(6) Yes, *let's do* that if you're thirsty.

(7) "Panda", it's the same word in English as in French.

(8) This ring ? It's *a gift from a friend of mine*.

(9) This tissue ? It's *to blow my nose with*, of course.

(10) No, it's *the first time* I've been away from home.

score : ... × 10 =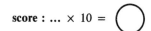

17. LES STRUCTURES VERBALES

A. LES CAUSATIFS : "FAIRE FAIRE"

a) Complétez ces phrases par make, have, get aux temps et aux formes voulus.

(1) A week ago, hijackers ... an Aeroflot pilot land in Stockholm.
(2) Try as you may, you ... him to listen to his mother's advice.
(3) This dress is very dirty, I ... it drycleaned tomorrow.
(4) She ... him slow down when they entered the village.
(5) When they arrived in America, immigrants ... (often) to change their names.
(6) She says she is not photogenic and refuses ... her picture taken.
(7) There's no ... Andrew go to bed before 11 o'clock.
(8) You are not to do that again. (I) ... myself understood ?

102 LES STRUCTURES VERBALES

   (9) Robin ... to put away his toys before he went out.
   (10) By announcing a 60-day amnesty, New York City's Mayor was trying ... people to turn in illegal firearms.

   score : ... × 10 = ◯

b) Traduisez ces phrases, en évitant le mot à mot.

   (1) Le directeur a fait visiter l'école aux pensionnaires.
   (2) Pourquoi leur as-tu fait peur ?
   (3) "Monsieur Lennox désire vous voir, Monsieur". "Faites-le entrer".
   (4) On ne fait pas attendre les dames.
   (5) As-tu fait réchauffer le ragoût ?
   (6) Fais-lui voir ton nouveau skateboard.
   (7) Elle a dû faire venir le médecin en pleine nuit.
   (8) Vous avez fait tomber votre gant.
   (9) Faites-nous savoir si vous voulez que l'on aille vous chercher à la gare.
   (10) Il s'est fait retirer son permis pour excès de vitesse.

   score : ... × 10 = ◯

c) Réécrivez les phrases en les transformant de façon à utiliser une structure causative (active ou passive) qui ait pour objet les mots en italiques.

   (1) *He* refused to open his suitcase when asked by the customs-officer.

LES STRUCTURES VERBALES

(2) He wants the police to arrest *his next-door neighbour* for indecent exposure.
He wants to ...

(3) No matter how hard I tried I couldn't persuade *him* to stop taking sleeping-pills.
No matter how hard I tried I couldn't...

(4) As he didn't pay his bills, *his phone* was disconnected.
As he didn't pay his bills, he...

(5) The Americans didn't build the Union Pacific Railway themselves. *The Chinese* built it.
The Americans...

(6) They must ask the decorator to finish painting *their flat* by the end of the week.
They must ...

(7) Being an actress, it was easy for *her* to cry anytime she wanted.
Being an actress, she could ...

(8) Every week, she pays the most expensive hairdresser to do *her hair*.
Every week, she ...

(9) Muslims won't let *anybody* enter a mosque if they don't take their shoes off.
Muslims...

(10) She wants the best oral surgeon to pull out *her tooth*.
She wants to ...

score : ... × 10 =

B. LA PROPOSITION INFINITIVE

a) Réécrivez ces phrases de façon à utiliser une proposition infinitive. Lorsque cela est nécessaire transformez le nom en pronom.

(1) She doesn't think *her guests* will arrive before 8 : 00.
She doesn't expect...
(2) *Dad* must always help Mum to do the washing-up.
Mum always wants...
(3) "*Elisa,* finish your homework before you watch TV".
She told...
(4) "Move back," the policeman ordered *the crowd*.
The policeman ordered...
(5) You shouldn't overwork yourself, he said to *me*.
He advised...
(6) "I sincerely hope you'll be happy, *Sandra*".
I sincerely wish...
(7) "Why don't *you and Tony* stop fighting and make up ?" Roy said.
Roy asked...
(8) They'd rather *Jason* didn't stay at his friend's house overnight.
They'd prefer...
(9) *We* won't have to change trains. It's an express train.
It won't be necessary...
(10) Don't let *the news* be known.
He doesn't want...

score : ... × 10 =

LES STRUCTURES VERBALES 105

b) A l'aide de l'amorce fournie, reformulez les phrases en utilisant une structure infinitive.

(1) "Here is some money for the fair, Steve, but don't go into the bumper-cars."
"Here is some money for the fair, Steve, but I don't want...

(2) The government must find a solution to the problem of drugs.
It is time ...

(3) In this advertisement, the adman's aim as regards the viewers is that they associate the atmosphere of refinement and luxury of this southern plantation with the product.
The adman wishes ...

(4) The sun is very hot today, I can't stay on the beach.
The sun is too hot ...

(5) You will have to check her address in the telephone-book.
It will be necessary ...

(6) They are lending their son money with which he will pay for his tuition and fees.
They are lending their son money ...

(7) He is so open-handed that everybody likes him.
He is open-handed enough ...

(8) We'll have a contract ready for you which you will be able to sign in a week.
We'll have a contract ready ...

(9) Your car is so small we won't all fit in.
Your car is too small ...

(10) If his son is in trouble, naturally he will be upset.
If his son is in trouble, it is natural ...

score : ... × 10 = ◯

C. STRUCTURES IDIOMATIQUES AVEC INVERSION

Remettez les éléments en ordre de façon à former une phrase cohérente.

(1) our / interested / contact / information / should / relations / about / further / you / our / department / please / be / in / product
(2) earned / matter / more / he / money / his / no / wife / always / he / hard / than / worked / how / did
(3) murderer / had / guessed / as / attention / was / the / I / more / reading / I / who / paid / was / I / have / detail / would / to
(4) may / come / try / would / as / not / he / sleep
(5) grand-parents / world / would / were / they / make / alive / the / today / of / what / my / ?
(6) solution / she / her / could / smart / problem / as / find / a / was / to / she / not
(7) hard / would / little / they / be / life / did / when / their / new / defected / how / know / they
(8) are / please / living / the / more / standard / the / of / the / enjoy / difficult / they / higher / people / to

(9) aged / come / never / abandon / what / my / will / may / parents / I
(10) working / than / rang / combination / no / the / alarm-system / on / sooner / started / robbers / had / the / safe / the

score : ... × 10 = ◯

D. TESTS RÉCAPITULATIFS

a) Mettez les verbes en italiques à la forme qui convient.

(1) Don't let Judy *to go out* at night alone.
(2) You should make her *to get dressed up* for her friend's birthday-party.
(3) Hadn't we better *to leave* the kids at home with a baby-sitter ?
(4) It's a shame that you *to be* so obstinate.
(5) I took my car to the garage for it *to check out* before I drove down to the Riviera.
(6) I wish the message I left on her answering-machine *not / to erase*.
(7) He was made *to change* his mind about women's rights.
(8) Do you object to Dan's *to spend* the night at his friend's house ?
(9) It won't be necessary for you *to forward* my mail while I am away.

(10) *you / to need* anything, don't hesitate to ask me.

score : ... × 10 = ◯

b) Trouvez dans la colonne B les phrases qui ont un lien logique avec celles de la colonne A.

A
- **(1)** She almost wished
- **(2)** You'd better
- **(3)** She'd like
- **(4)** He made
- **(5)** Teachers resent

B
- **(a)** her son to make his career in teaching.
- **(b)** she had never met him or even heard of him.
- **(c)** their pupils chewing gum during class.
- **(d)** her move to London and settle there with him.
- **(e)** resign after your bad results in the election.

score : ... × 20 = ◯

c) Même exercice.

A
- **(1)** I wish
- **(2)** She won't forgive
- **(3)** He'd rather

LES STRUCTURES VERBALES

(4) The union-leader had
(5) There's seldom a good reason

B

(a) his wife spent less money on clothes.
(b) her for letting her down when she was in need.
(c) for your being absent from class.
(d) you wouldn't use curse words so often.
(e) all the petitions signed by all the members.

score : ... × 20 = ◯

d) Trouvez la solution qui ne convient pas.

(1) What about / They feel like / They see no objection to / Let's / cancelling the picnic, since the weather isn't good enough.
(2) I can't stand / I could see them / I don't want / There's no point queueing at the bus-stop.
(3) He'll get him / He'd better / He made him / He needn't find a quick solution to his problem.
(4) She'd like / She would enjoy / She wants / She was made to express herself freely on the subject.
(5) I expected / I wished / I'd rather / I wondered why my son hadn't taken after his father.

score : ... × 20 = ◯

e) Traduisez.

(1) Elle aurait mieux fait de contrôler que le gaz était fermé avant de quitter la maison.
(2) Elles se sont fait attaquer par un jeune drogué.
(3) Je n'ai pas pu lui faire dire la vérité.
(4) Il les a fait mettre de côté pour toi.
(5) Je souhaiterais que nous soyons déjà demain soir.
(6) Jeremy, je souhaiterais que tu laisses ton frère tranquille.
(7) Il préférerait que tu ne lui poses pas de questions sur le détail de ses activités d'hier.
(8) Je préférerais ne pas voir sa réaction quand il apprendra que nous possédons 4 voitures.
(9) Tu ne peux pas vraiment t'attendre à ce que ton patron t'accorde plus de trois semaines de congé.
(10) Elle attendait avec impatience que son mari soit en retraite pour pouvoir voyager.

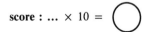

score : ... × 10 =

18. L'EXCLAMATION

a) Complétez en utilisant how, what, such, so, suivis du déterminant qui convient (a, an, ∅).

(1) ... enthusiastic he sounded !
(2) She is ... avid skier that she would travel miles to find good slopes !
(3) ... fright you gave me !
(4) ... dull people your neighbours are !
(5) "My father is an entomologist" "Oh, is he ? ... interesting !
(6) Everybody enjoyed the concert. It was ... brilliant performance !
(7) ... heavy the traffic was this morning !
(8) ... day we've had !
(9) He is ... heavy smoker !
(10) Why did you have to say that ? ... thoughtless of you !

score : ... × 10 = ◯

b) Transformez ces phrases de façon à produire des phrases exclamatives.

(1) You've got a romantic turn of mind.
(2) It was clever of you.
(3) All the girls are fond of him. He is a good-looking fellow.

112 L'EXCLAMATION

- **(4)** It was an ordeal.
- **(5)** This child really reads well.
- **(6)** You make me feel totally inadequate.
- **(7)** It was a delicious meal, thank you.
- **(8)** It was nice seeing you again.
- **(9)** That's a car !
- **(10)** He acted very stupidly.

score : ... × 10 =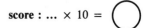

19. LE PASSIF

a) Mettez le verbe en italiques à la forme qui convient.

(1) In 1964, America *to tear* by violence and unrest.
(2) This hedge needs trimming. It does, it *to do* tomorrow.
(3) Did you know Tom had been promoted ? Yes, I *to tell-just*.
(4) Is your car ready ? Not yet, it *to service-still*.
(5) *to bring up - should* boys and girls the same way ?
(6) He *to lock up* for 13 years when he was pardoned.
(7) This photograph *to take-must* in Italy during her honeymoon.
(8) Passengers *to request - now* by some airlines to refrain from smoking.
(9) *to attend to* you ?
(10) Many years ago, blacks *to deny - used to* the right to vote.

score : ... × 10 = ◯

b) Mettez les phrases suivantes au passif. Ne mettez le complément d'agent que si cela est nécessaire.

(1) Why didn't you teach those children good manners ?

114 LE PASSIF

- **(2)** The porter will take care of your luggage.
- **(3)** They had told me only part of the truth.
- **(4)** People contract cholera and typhoid by drinking infected water.
- **(5)** The government is bound to tear down all the slums in this area one day.
- **(6)** The postman has already collected the mail.
- **(7)** They are shooting a film about the Sahara.
- **(8)** They will forward my mail to me.
- **(9)** Someone should talk the workers into going back to work.
- **(10)** Did the secretary tell him to come back later ?

score : ... × 10 = ◯

c) Même exercice.

- **(1)** His son took over his business.
- **(2)** They will publish his book next month.
- **(3)** They refused him entry into the Opera House.
- **(4)** They told him not to make a rude remark.
- **(5)** He made her slow down on arriving in the village.
- **(6)** They may ask her husband to testify in her favour.
- **(7)** The radio said the weather would be cold and rainy tomorrow.
- **(8)** Many people regard Washington as the greatest of all presidents.
- **(9)** Could they make him confess his crimes ?
- **(10)** Did the police arrest any of the demonstrators ?

(11) People assume he worked for the CIA.
(12) They suppose they will reduce pollution drastically by the end of the year 2000.
(13) Penguins are relatively friendly animals that one can approach easily.
(14) Many people think that money is the root of all evil.
(15) They are building a dam on the Danube to generate electricity.
(16) American restaurants often provide patrons with doggie-bags.
(17) Nobody likes people to boss them around.
(18) They awarded him the Nobel Prize for physics.
(19) Nobody will know the extent of the damage until the flood has receded.
(20) People think she is a drug-addict.

score : ... × 5 = ◯

d) Complétez les phrases à l'aide d'un des éléments proposés.

(1) Kennedy **was killed / got killed / has been killed / has to be killed** by Oswald.
(2) Illegitimate children **are frowned at / are frowned / are frowned upon / are frowned upon them** by society.
(3) You **are being wanted / are to be wanted / will be wanted / are wanted** downstairs at once.
(4) San Francisco **is said to be / is said / is said it is / is told to be** the most beautiful city in America.

(5) He **is thought to be educated / is thought to have been educated / is thought that he was educated / is thought of being educated** at Eton.

(6) Her neighbours **have been heard quarrel / have been heard to quarrel / are heard quarrelling / are heard to quarrel** for over an hour.

(7) Please do as you **are said. / are being said. / are told to. / are told.**

(8) Pilots **are made work / are made working / are made to work / have them worked** for as many hours as can be squeezed out of them.

(9) You'll be surprised when you **are told / will be told / shall be told / be told** what they think about you.

(10) What is **to do with her ? / she to be done with ? / to be done with her ? / she done with ?**

score : ... × 10 =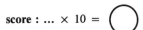

20. LE DISCOURS INDIRECT

a) Mettez ces phrases au discours indirect.

" **(1)** I really enjoy myself a lot **(2)** whenever I go skating," she said.

" **(3)** I met my husband while running the New York Marathon," she remarked.

" **(4)** What on earth are you doing here, **(5)** and what are you up to ?" he inquired.

" **(6)** Can you do me a favour Eva ?" he asked.

" **(7)** We're afraid **(8)** we'll have to be going, **(9)** it's late," they told her.

"**(10)** Cancel all my appointments for the afternoon **(11)** and don't disturb me for the next 30 minutes," he ordered his secretary.

"**(12)** As soon as I am granted my fellowship, **(13)** I'll start working on my Ph. D. Dissertation," he told me.

"**(14)** Do you intend to do some sightseeing **(15)** when you are in Canada ?" they asked us.

"**(16)** It's the easiest thing in the world to give up smoking, **(17)** I have done it a hundred times," he remarked.

"**(18)** It's an emergency, **(19)** you must come right away," he said.

118 LE DISCOURS INDIRECT

"**(20)** How long will you be teaching in South Carolina ?" she asked.

score : ... × 5 = ◯

b) Mettez ces phrases au discours indirect.

" **(1)** You mustn't pick flowers in public parks," the gardener told the children.

" **(2)** Shall I wait for a taxi or take the bus, **(3)** I really don't know," he said.

" **(4)** Don't worry, **(5)** we'll find our way back to the hotel," they told the clerk at the desk.

" **(6)** Let's have a look at their rose garden," he suggested.

" **(7)** Well, it's many years **(8)** since we first met. **(9)** How time flies ! **(10)** Do you remember **(11)** the first time I saw you ?" he asked.

"**(12)** I may be going down to the country this weekend, **(13)** and if I do, **(14)** I won't be back until next week," she informed them.

"**(15)** Can you make it to our party tomorrow ?" he asked her.

"**(16)** He has a heart condition, **(17)** and he knows **(18)** something may happen to him. **(19)** All these months he's been living under a death sentence and failing to take any of the precautions **(20)** that might commute it," she told me.

score : ... × 5 = ◯

LE DISCOURS INDIRECT

c) Complétez ces phrases à l'aide d'une des solutions proposées.

(1) The child wanted to find out how **lived cowboys. / did cowboys live. / cowboys lived.**

(2) They felt sure they **must be delayed / must have been delayed / must have delayed** at the customs.

(3) They announced that their new product **would be launched / will be launched / had been launched** on the market by the end of the year.

(4) Our Italian friends wanted to know whether we **may be flying / may fly / would be flying** to Europe during the summer.

(5) They wondered where **the new shopping centre was. / was the new shopping centre. / was there a new shopping centre.**

(6) She told him he **didn't call / needn't have called / mustn't have called** the restaurant to make a reservation, she had already called them.

(7) I asked them what they would be doing **the following day. / the day after next. / tomorrow.**

(8) He admitted he **would let me know / should have let me know / should let me know** earlier he was dining out.

(9) She explained that she **won't have to save / needn't save / didn't have to save** money to send her son to College since he had dropped out of high school.

(10) He declared he had retired from the Navy **3 years before and had been growing / last year and had grown / 3 years ago and had been growing** orchids in Florida ever since.

score : ... × 10 = ◯

120 LE DISCOURS INDIRECT

d) Mettez ces phrases au discours direct.

He told me **(1)** that he had worked for two years in a Cleveland Office **(2)** before he was transferred to the New York headquarters.
He asked her **(3)** why she had had her boyfriend murdered.
She thought **(4)** her boss was wearing a very elegant suit that day.
They told her **(5)** she was wrong to get upset about little things.
She suggested **(6)** they should do their Christmas shopping early this year.
When I asked my friend what to do she answered **(7)** I had better tell them the truth.
The nurse wondered **(8)** whether the child had had the measles immunization or not.
She advised him **(9)** to return the wallet **(10)** he had found to the police station.
He told his real estate agent **(11)** that he had been trying to reach him for the last three days.
She ordered him **(12)** to run down to the shop on the corner, **(13)** to get her a dozen eggs and not to break them.
She wanted to know **(14)** how long they had been taking violin lessons.
The clerk told him **(15)** he didn't have to bring the forms back before the following week.
He explained to me **(16)** that when he went to college **(17)** he would share an apartment with a room-mate.
During her holiday in Switzerland she often said **(18)** that she wished **(19)** she had been able to go hang-gliding.

LE DISCOURS INDIRECT 121

She apologized to her parents **(20)** for being nosy.

score : ... × 5 = ◯

e) Mettez les textes suivants au discours indirect.

"**(1)** Why do you keep reading your Bible all day long ?" a youngster asked his aged granny.
"**(2)** Honey," she answered, "you might say **(3)** I was cramming for my final examinations."

A hypocritical Boston tycoon once told Mark Twain, "**(4)** Before I die **(5)** I mean to make a pilgrimage to the top of Mount Sinai in the Holy Land, and read the Ten Commandments aloud." "**(6)** Why don't you stay right home in Boston and keep them ?"

Mrs Beamish called to her husband, "**(7)** Last year we sent Mother a chair. **(8)** What do you think **(9)** we ought to do for her this year ?" Mr Beamish called back, "**(10)** Electrify it."

"**(11)** I think **(12)** you ought to stop taking sleeping pills every night," a doctor warned an ageing star. "**(13)** They're habit-forming."
"**(14)** Don't be a drip," she told him. "**(15)** I've been taking them for 20 years now, **(16)** and they haven't become a habit yet !"

A housewife complained constantly to her husband about the apartment they lived in. "**(17)** All our friends live ten times better than we do," she said. "**(18)** We simply must move into a more expensive neighbourhood." One night her long-suffering husband came home and told her, "**(19)** Well, we don't have to move after all. **(20)** The landlord just doubled our rent."

score : ... $\times\ 5\ =\ \bigcirc$

21. LE GROUPE VERBAL : RÉVISION GÉNÉRALE

a) Mettez les verbes en italiques au temps et à la forme voulus.

After a hundred years of existence, basketball **(1)** *to become* one of the most popular spectator sports in the US.

If I **(2)** *to know* how to get in touch with her, I would send her a wedding-invitation.

As soon as I **(3)** *to finish* unblocking the sink, I'll have a look at your washing-machine.

When he was in the south of France during the war, all he thought about was **(4)** *to get* home alive.

When the atomic bombs **(5)** *to fall* on Hiroshima and Nagasaki 45 years ago, they killed 150,000 people instantly.

"You **(6)** *modal + to have* the car tonight." Then he caught himself abruptly and said, "No, you **(7)** *modal + to have* it, I need it myself."

When he came back from Vietnam after the war, he felt he **(8)** *to lose* both his fear of death and his respect for life.

My grand-father who **(9)** *to be* 80 this year, is still leading a very active life.

I **(10)** *modal + to know* what I was in for, as soon as I saw my parents' face.

He **(11)** *to think* of marrying her when she eloped with an elderly millionaire.

When she had her tonsils removed, she **(12)** *to have to* stay in hospital for one week.

Since she had become a famous actress, her friends **(13)** *to treat* her with exaggerated deference.

If her parents hadn't been so strict with her, she **(14)** *to run away* from home.

When the Prince of Wales **(15)** *to become* King, he will be the official head of state and the head of the Church of England.

For the Queen Mum's birthday The Royal Mint **(16)** *to strike* a one-pound collector's coin.

Japanese businessmen see hard work as a prerequisite to **(17)** *to achieve* any business success.

The Procope, the oldest café in Paris, **(18)** *to operate* ever since 1686.

If she has a baby now, she **(19)** *to have to* leave her job and her whole future **(20)** *to disrupt*.

score : ... × 5 = ◯

b) Même exercice.

"An epidemic of extinction **(1)** *to begin*. Every hour a unique species of plant or animal **(2)** *to disappear* from the face of the earth (...) and the rate of loss **(3)** *to accelerate*. Before the 20th century **(4)** *to be* out, millions of species **(5)** *to vanish* for ever." *(Ark Manifesto)*

"In a hundred years," Virginia Woolf **(6)** *to predict* in the 1920s, "the nursemaid **(7)** *to heave* coal. The shopwoman **(8)** *to drive* an engine."

Ever since Dick Tracy first **(9)** *to use* his wrist radio **(10)** *to nail* thugs in the 1930s, the communications industry **(11)** *to dream* of **(12)** *to provide* everyone with a tiny personal communicator.

Ever since they **(13)** *to start* their westward migration from India eight centuries ago, Gypsies **(14)** *to face* discrimination and prejudice. Half a million **(15)** *to die* in Nazi concentration camps ; tattooed Zs, for Zigeuner (Gypsy in German), **(16)** *to be* still visible on the arms of many holocaust survivors. They **(17)** *often/to associate* with fortune-telling and begging or thieving... And yet they **(18)** *to contribute* to Europe's history for 500 years. Today Gypsy scholars and activists **(19)** *to bicker* over how best **(20)** *to integrate* Gypsies into the new Europe.

score : ... × 5 = ◯

c) Même exercice.

"The Tube" **(1)** *to become* everyone's favourite metaphor for England's decline.
The Evening Standard **(2)** *to call* London's underground rail system a "human sewer" and **(3)** *to ride* it a "near-death experience". No wonder J. Riezeck, an American film-maker, **(4)** *to choose* the London Tube when he

(5) *to seek* the world's slowest, filthiest subway for the setting of his new film.

In recent months, London passengers (6) *to have* even more reason to complain. A few months ago fares (7) *to go up* by more than 10 %, which means that it now (8) *to cost* commuters 70 pence for a ride in central London. That (9) *to make* London's Underground the most expensive in Europe.

Even though it (10) *to be* the world's oldest subway system, it (11) *never / properly / to modernize* since it (12) *to build* over a century ago. Everyone (13) *to remember* the 1987 King's Cross escalator fire which (14) *to kill* 31 people. The reason is that for four decades successive governments (15) *to neglect* to cope with the problem.

(16) *to protest* against wooden escalators, overcrowding and inadequate protection against fire, riders (17) *to stage* a series of sit-down strikes in the stations...

It is essential that the government (18) *to take* rapid measures to improve the existing conditions of the London Tube.

The only advantage one (19) *modal + to find* in travelling the tube today is that crime (20) *actually / to fall* !

score : ... × 5 = 〇

d) Trouvez dans la colonne B les phrases qui ont un lien logique avec celles de la colonne A.

(i) **A**

(1) If you go jogging every day
(2) If you went jogging every day

(3) Whenever you went jogging every day
(4) Since you go jogging every day
(5) If you had gone jogging every day

B

(a) you remained fit.
(b) you remain fit.
(c) you will remain fit.
(d) you would have remained fit.
(e) you would remain fit.

(ii)   **A**

(1) That's the limit Sophie, I wish
(2) I strongly resent
(3) I did not hear you
(4) Don't expect him
(5) Whether you want to or not,

B

(a) calling us in.
(b) I had left you back home.
(c) you'll have to go to the army.
(d) his minding my business.
(e) to be grateful to you.

score : ... × 10 = ◯

e) Traduisez ces phrases.

(1) Es-tu déjà allé en Irlande ?
(2) Plus il vieillissait, plus il devenait chauve.

128 LE GROUPE VERBAL

   (3) Il faut que tu t'occupes de cet enfant.
   (4) Lui as-tu demandé ce qu'elle faisait depuis une heure ?
   (5) Vous ne devriez pas manger tant de viande.
   (6) On m'a volé ma voiture.
   (7) Pourquoi t'es-tu fait couper les cheveux ?
   (8) Je ne sais pas combien coûte ce livre.
   (9) Il a aidé un aveugle à traverser la rue.
(10) Il se pourrait que ce magasin soit fermé.

score : ... × 10 = ◯

f) Traduisez ces phrases.

   (1) Vous n'avez pas besoin de vous dépêcher.
   (2) Elle n'a pas compris ce que tu lui as dit, moi non plus.
   (3) Ne t'attends pas à ce qu'elle soit à l'heure.
   (4) Il se conduit comme s'il était le patron.
   (5) Voilà longtemps que nous n'avons pas eu de neige en hiver.
   (6) Quand elle était au Japon, elle ne s'est jamais habituée à manger du poisson cru.
   (7) Tu ne m'écoutes pas, à quoi penses-tu ?
   (8) Que veux-tu faire quand tu seras grand ?
   (9) Il a du être surpris par l'accueil chaleureux qu'on lui a réservé.
(10) Il se peut qu'il ait déjà envoyé sa pellicule à développer.

score : ... × 10 = ◯

22. LES PRÉPOSITIONS

A. LES PRÉPOSITIONS DE LIEU

a) Complétez ce texte par des prépositions.

Shortly after midnight, a fire broke out **(1)** ... the second floor of a private house **(2)** ... Park Street. Ten minutes later fire alarms could be heard ringing **(3)** ... the area.
When the fire-brigade arrived, high flames were coming **(4)** ... the ground-floor French windows, and were already reaching **(5)** ... the first-floor windows. Inside the house people were scurrying **(6)** ... the smoke-filled hall and **(7)** ... the front garden. **(8)** ..., **(9)** ... the second-floor, a woman was yelling at the top of her lungs and was about to jump **(10)** ... one of the windows. As the firemen couldn't get **(11)** ... the house **(12)** ... the door which had collapsed **(13)** ... the front steps, by the time they got there, they put up the extending ladder and took her out **(14)** ... the window. **(15)** ... the street **(16)** ... the little house some people were **(17)** ... their windows. Others were watching **(18)** ... their gardens. There were people standing all **(19)** ... the street. By half-past two the firemen had managed to

control the fire. Nothing much remained of the house except rubble and a thick cloud of smoke hanging **(20)** ... the house.

score : ... × 5 = ◯

B. AUTRES PRÉPOSITIONS

a) Complétez par des prépositions ou par ∅.

(1) Most of the violence shown ... TV and in films today is gratuitous.
(2) I can't listen ... two people at a time.
(3) Did you tell ... your friend that he had good write-ups in the local papers ?
(4) In America if you can't drive a car, you're dependent ... your parents to drive you around.
(5) Los Angeles was very different ... what I expected.
(6) Who are you going to borrow a skateboard ... ?
(7) The New York stock exchange is one of the largest stock markets ... the world.
(8) You should knock before entering ... my study.
(9) Shall we meet next ... the telephone booth which is opposite **(10)** ... the chemist's ?
(11) You're likely to get ... trouble if you're rude.
(12) More than 30,000 people die each year in the UK ... lung cancer.
(13) You must come ... dinner one of these days.
(14) Do you think he'll marry ... this elderly woman ?

LES PRÉPOSITIONS 131

(15) It's a child's duty to look ... his or her parents when they're old.
(16) When they were away ... holiday, they did nothing but eat and sleep.
(17) His car went off the road and crashed ... a tree.
(18) A gang of delinquents mugged an old woman and robbed her ... all her valuables.
(19) Did you ask ... the waiter if Annie had already paid **(20)** ... the drinks ?
(21) They always go to Midnight Mass ... Christmas Eve.
(22) They were discussing ... the financial impact of the unification of Germany.
(23) Did your neighbours call ... you **(24)** ... Sunday ?
(25) Why shouldn't I be interested ... genealogy ? A great many people are.

score : ... × 4 = ◯

b) Choisissez la préposition qui convient.

(1) They should be back **during / by / at / on** next week.
(2) An anti-vivisection group has been held responsible **of / about / for / to** attacks on the homes of doctors and scientists.
(3) They are not alone **by / to / in / Ø** being impressed by glasnost.
(4) "Operator, please, can you put me **through / to / across / on**."

LES PRÉPOSITIONS

(5) He was charged **on / with / of / Ø** the murder of his twelve cats !

(6) Child abuse is **in / on / at /about** the increase in many countries.

(7) My god mother sent me a cheque **for / on / of / about** £ 50 for my birthday.

(8) It's a long time since I heard **from / Ø / of / on** my friends in the Netherlands.

(9) Mother kangaroos have a special pocket to carry their baby **into / out of / in / on**.

(10) Advertisers tend to cater **Ø / to / for / on** young people's tastes.

(11) What shall I wear **to / at / on / in** the Turners' on Saturday night ?

(12) They encountered hardships, but not the kind they had planned **about / on / Ø / for**.

(13) Many Third World countries which suffer ... malnutrition, are eager to share ... world prosperity. **(of-in / from-to / from-in / of-to)**

(14) The inflation rate could jump from 2.6% to 4% **within / during / throughout / for** 2 years if the situation doesn't improve.

(15) Many ecologists have called **for / Ø / to / on** international action to cope with the problems of the greenhouse effect and global warming.

(16) How can one be indifferent **at / to / about / for** poverty and homelessness ?

(17) The government recently agreed ... a 1.5% increase ... university spending. **(at-of / to-of / to-in / Ø-in)**

(18) His parents tried to persuade him ... apply ... a temporary job. **(to-Ø / into-for / into-Ø / to-for)**

(19) Don't insist **to / on / about / Ø** telling a good joke after your audience informs you they have heard it.

(20) How many classes did you attend **at / to / Ø / in** when you were in summer school ?

(21) Whenever you put out a half-smoked cigarette you prolong your life **by / of / for / Ø** 10 minutes.

(22) In 1896, 13 nations participated ... the first Olympics which took place ... Athens. **(to-to / in-in / at-at / into-in)**

(23) Do you stay at the Hilton when you go **to / for / on / in** a business trip ?

(24) The beggar thanked her **about / of / for / on** the note she put into his hat.

(25) Do you support **for / Ø / against / to** nuclear disarmament ?

score : ... × 4 = ◯

c) Traduisez en évitant le mot à mot.

(1) He kicked the door open.
(2) You can't walk to the drug-store, it's too far. You'd better drive.
(3) He talked her into taking fencing lessons with him.
(4) He was stabbed to death on a deserted street in Chicago.
(5) She squeezed the lemon dry, then added water and sugar.
(6) I had a terrible headache but I slept it off.

- **(7)** Don't ever run across a street.
- **(8)** He elbowed his way through the crowd.
- **(9)** The boy-scouts canoed down the Colorado River.
- **(10)** They laughed the ghost out of the house.

d) Traduisez.

- **(1)** Ne vous penchez pas à la fenêtre.
- **(2)** Je n'aime pas boire dans le verre de quelqu'un d'autre.
- **(3)** C'est quoi ton sac ? Du cuir ?
- **(4)** Retire les mains de tes poches.
- **(5)** Comment traduiriez-vous cette expression en anglais ?
- **(6)** Servez-vous de fruits.
- **(7)** Je m'achèterai un sandwich dans le train.
- **(8)** Entrez, je vous en prie.
- **(9)** A quel étage habites-tu ?
- **(10)** Elle vit dans un ranch au Texas.

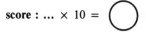

23. LES MOTS DE LIAISON

a) **Complétez ces phrases avec un des mots proposés. Attention, dans l'une de ces phrases c'est la solution qui ne convient pas que vous devez trouver.**

(1) **Until / Once / Unless / No sooner** you've made up your mind to do something, you shouldn't indulge in second thoughts.

(2) He became interested in volcanoes **when / once / until / whenever** he was working in Africa as a geologist.

(3) She intends to bring up her son and her daughter in the same way **for fear that / so that / so as to / lest** avoid having another male chauvinist in the family.

(4) **As far as / Even if / Whereas / Whether** we'll be able to give you a hand depends on what day you are moving.

(5) **Unless / No sooner / Until / Hardly** will drugs be legalized than drug-barons and drug-dealers will be out of business.

(6) **As soon as / Since / As far as / Once** I can remember, Howard Hughes was a Texan tycoon.

(7) **No matter / However / Whatever / Whether** how many invitations for lunch and dinner I receive, I turn them all down.

- **(8) Whenever / No sooner / While / Hardly** had the aircraft taken off, when one of the engines caught fire.
- **(9)** Stories of pilots falling asleep in the cockpit are common **as long as / provided / even if / whereas** the public doesn't always hear about them.
- **(10) Once / Although / Whether / Unless** the government takes drastic measures, the inflation rate will continue to soar.
- **(11) Unless / While / As / In spite of** she fiercely wished she were a man, at the same time she hated men.
- **(12)** I don't mind if you turn on the radio **provided / though / as long as / as** you don't tune in to rock music.
- **(13)** There seems to be a law of life that we don't appreciate something **as far as / until / whether / though** we no longer have it.
- **(14)** Turn on the answering machine **in case / in order to / so as to / provided** someone should call you while you're away.
- **(15)** He decided to take a sabbatical **as long as / so that / in order to / in case** devote more time to research.
- **(16)** Hanging won't be reintroduced in England **so that / for fear that / as far as / as long as** innocent people should lose their lives.
- **(17) Whereas / Since / Whatever / Even though** the accused had good alibis, they were sentenced to life imprisonment.
- **(18)** He studied at a good university for several years **whereas / in spite of / provided / whether** his father was a self-made man.

(19) You may borrow my camera **unless / provided / until / once** you take good care of it.

(20) We can stay up and watch the late programme **as / in case / whereas / whether** tomorrow is Sunday.

score : ... × 5 =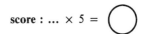

) **Rédigez une seule phrase à partir des deux éléments proposés en utilisant les mots de liaison ci-dessous.**

(i) in order to - provided - although - no sooner - whenever

(1) He got the star role in a horror film. Soon he became very rich and very famous.
(2) He came back quite late. However dinner was waiting for him on the table.
(3) We might decide to rent this big house. The price mustn't be too high.
(4) The Americans dropped an atomic bomb on Hiroshima. They wanted to get the Japanese to surrender.
(5) They are together. They always get into big arguments.

(ii) whereas - until - as - hardly - so that

(6) The general public won't pay much attention to ecological problems. A serious accident must occur first.

138 LES MOTS DE LIAISON

(7) Let me have your phone number. I can get in touch with you.
(8) American comics have traditionally been written for children. On the contrary French comics are read by adults as well.
(9) The clock struck twelve. Cinderella's coach immediately vanished into thin air.
(10) He came down with flu. He had to stay in bed for a week.

score : ... × 10 = ◯

c) Trouvez les phrases du groupe B qui vont avec celles du groupe A et reliez-les entre elles avec les mots de liaison ci-dessous.

(i) unless - as soon as - until - while - so as not to

A

(1) I'll have to walk to the office
(2) He pursued his studies
(3) She lived at home
(4) The new parliament will be in session
(5) He tiptoed into the house

B

(a) she was of age.
(b) the elections are over.

(c) you're willing to give me a ride.
(d) wake up anybody.
(e) working as a taxi-driver.

(ii) for fear - whenever - whereas - provided - although

A

(6) He drives to work every day
(7) She's an early riser
(8) I am always out
(9) You won't get into trouble
(10) She bought an alarm-system for her car

B

(f) the postman comes with a telegram.
(g) his licence has been revoked.
(h) you don't do anything illegal.
(i) a thief should steal it.
(j) I am a late sleeper.

score : ... × 10 = ◯

24. LES NOMBRES

a) Réécrivez les nombres en toutes lettres.

She is on the wrong side of **(1)** 40.
(2) 113 prisoners escaped last year.
Trains collided : **(3)** 206 killed, **(4)** 750 injured.
He owns **(5)** 3,500 heads of cattle.
(6) 90,002 hold lunar reservations on PAN AM.
(7) 30,600 demonstrators took their protest onto the street.
(8) 582,730 immigrants are legally admitted into the US every year.
Has the population of China reached **(9)** 1,000,000,000 ?
In **(10)** 1989 there were **(11)** 1,008,000,000 inhabitants.
In **(12)** 1985 Bolivia had a **(13)** 15,000 % inflation rate.
Recently prices have gone up by **(14)** 0.7%.
(15) Elizabeth I, daughter of **(16)** Henry VIII, died in **(17)** 1603.
The Aral sea, once the world's **(18)** 6th largest sea, has lost **(19)** 2/3 of its volume already.
Yesterday the temperature was in the **(20)** 80s.

score : ... × 5 =

b) Même exercice.

Take the **(1)** 8 : 15 train.
He left Germany before **(2)** World War II.
The entrance to the Met is on **(3)** 5th Avenue.
Water freezes at **(4)** 0° C.
This is a *Newsweek* article dated January **(5)** 15, **(6)** 1990.
Last year McDonald's had **(7)** $ 14.3 billion in sales.
For further information call : **(8)** 212 732 60 55.
Here is my new address : **(9)** 1249 Riverside Drive, New York, **(10)** 10024 NY.
English is spoken by at least **(11)** 750 million people.
Is the hippie movement a phenomenon of the **(12)** 50s or the **(13)** 60s ?
There are **(14)** 450,000 entries in *Webster's Dictionary*.
The number of tourists visiting Asian countries should increase by **(15)** 50 % by the year **(16)** 2000.
Is your licence plate number **(17)** 532 718 Y ?
What will the world be like in the **(18)** 21st century ?
(19) 300,000 at abortion rally on Sunday, March **(20)** 12.

score : ... × 5 = ◯

25. HANDLE WITH CARE !

A. TO MAKE - TO DO

a) **Complétez en utilisant les verbes** to make **ou** to do **aux temps et aux formes voulus.**

Men often boast that anything women can (1) ... they can (2) ... better. This, evidently, doesn't include (3) ... the housework. What's more they also wonder why housewives (4) ... such a fuss over nothing. If they (5) ... money or just (6) ... ends meet, they (7) ... it clear that since their wives don't work and consequently don't (8) ... a living, women have the time to (9) ... all the chores, i.e. (10) ... the washing-up, (11) ... the beds and (12) ... the laundry.

And yet some men (13) ... an effort and (14) ... the shopping on Saturday mornings, thinking that this (15) ... it, (16) ... sure all the while that everybody hears about their feat !

In the evening, while the kids (17) ... their homework, men (18) ... themselves comfortable in front of the television, waiting for their wives who (19) ... wonders in the kitchen and (20) ... their very best to (21) ... everybody happy. And this (22) ... a housewife's day !

(23) ... a long story short, what can one (24) ... of all this ? As far as the housework is concerned, the best thing for women is (25) ... without men !

score : ... × 4 =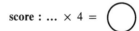

b) Choisissez la solution qui convient.

(1) I forgot the appointment I **had done** / **had made** / **had had** / **had taken** with the ophtalmologist.
(2) Mother wants me to **say** / **make** / **do** / **tell** my prayers every night before going to sleep.
(3) I **did** / **dreamed** / **made** / **had** a nightmare last night.
(4) That'll **make** / **go** / **do** / **work** for the moment, thank you.
(5) I have to go to the post-office to **give** / **do** / **make** / **hold** my phone call. My line is out of order.
(6) **Make** / **Let** / **Do** / **Have** me know when you are ready, I'll come and pick you up.
(7) Since he didn't understand the question, he **made** / **said** / **did** / **played** a joke of it.
(8) Can you **do** / **make** / **exchange** / **get** the change for this twenty-dollar bill please ?
(9) She was dressed to kill that night and really didn't **make** / **do** / **show up** / **show** her age.
(10) I think you **are doing** / **are giving** / **are making** / **are taking** her more credit than she deserves.

score : ... × 10 =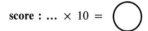

c) Trouvez dans la colonne B les phrases qui ont un lien logique avec celles de la colonne A.

(i)   **A**

(1) It won't do
(2) Could you please do
(3) I have done
(4) He had always thought that his job would have something to do
(5) Why did you do

B

(a) your hair in this braided dreadlocks style ?
(b) any good crying over spilt milk.
(c) me a favour ?
(d) better than I had ever hoped or dreamed I might do.
(e) with the movies.

(ii)   **A**

(1) It doesn't make
(2) He took a taxi to the station, but didn't make
(3) Can you make
(4) The script was so mediocre that he had to make
(5) Who made

B

(a) sure you didn't lock out the cat.
(b) any difference what time you come back.
(c) that film about the Woodstock festival ?
(d) it on time.
(e) do with a second-rate director and actors.

score : ... × 10 =

HANDLE WITH CARE ! 145

B. TO SAY - TO TELL

Complétez en utilisant les verbes to say **ou** to tell **aux temps et aux formes voulus**.

It often **(1)** ... that fortunetellers are crooks and that one shouldn't believe everything they **(2)** ... when they **(3)** ... you your future. **(4)** ... the truth, I don't quite agree with this and moreover, I don't care what people **(5)** ... I must admit I even went to see one. After all you never can **(6)** ..., she might have interesting things **(7)** ... me about myself and my future. I thought I needn't **(8)** ... anyone and of course, she **(9)** ... on me.

She was a surly woman, **(10)** ... the least, and her age was beginning **(11)** ... . "In your love line," she **(12)** ... "I'm sorry **(13)** ... , I see you've just missed the woman of your life. She was sitting opposite you on the bus a few days ago. But something **(14)** ... me you'll be travelling on that same bus and ..." Then she **(15)** ... that as far as my life line was concerned, I would live to be an old man, that is **(16)** ... to the age of 96, surrounded by 60 children and grand-children. She also **(17)** ... me I wouldn't be a failure and would manage to make ends meet.

Dumbfounded, I **(18)** ... good-bye and left, remembering, but too late, the proverb that **(19)** ... : "The truth is sometimes best left **(20)** ..."

score : ... × 5 = ◯

C. LES FAUX-AMIS

a) **Choisissez parmi les solutions proposées celle qui correspond à la définition du mot ou de l'expression en italiques.**

(1) As a rule I celebrate Christmas with my *relations* **relatives / acquaintances / neighbours and friends**.
(2) She worked for a while playing small parts in films, but *presently* **immediately / soon / at the time** she was out of work again.
(3) Bats are commonly *regarded as* **looked at / considered / looked down on** unattractive ugly creatures.
(4) Many years ago, before the highway was built, there was only *a wagon-trail* **a railway-track / a switch / a path for carts and carriages** here.
(5) Given the necessary opportunity, this *versatile* **talented / capricious / moody** man might have done well in any one field.
(6) There was no point making a fuss over such a *trivial* **obscene / petty / boring** mistake.
(7) He wanted to leave his wife and made up his mind that he would do so *eventually* **finally / probably / possibly.**
(8) After her child's death, she was very unhappy and resented her friends' *sympathy* **affection / congenial attitude / compassion.**
(9) *The deception in her voice was obvious* **It was evident that she was trying to cheat me / Listening to her, it was evident that she was disillusioned / Her disappointment was evident**. I couldn't be taken in.

HANDLE WITH CARE ! 147

(10) Most Americans strongly *question any assumption* **ask the reason why / don't accept the fact / doubt the fact** that ten years from now, the Japanese will be more powerful than the US.

score : ... × 10 = ◯

b) Remettez les éléments en ordre de façon à reconstituer une phrase cohérente. Dans chaque phrase un élément doit être omis.

(1) European / drug-addiction / the / nowadays / on / many / actually / in / is / today / rise / countries

(2) diary / she / bottom / her / drawer / study / keeps / of / desk / in / her / the

(3) number / will / platform / your / 3 / leaving / quay / from / train / be

(4) restaurant / cook / in / has / he / long / the / is / had / best / cooker / time / a / this

(5) second-hand / street / down / little / she / library / the / always / in /her / the / buys / books / book-shop

(6) because / Stenvenson / wear / old / 's / jacket / Louis / he / Robert / surname / "Velvet coat" / liked / nickname / an / velvet / to / was

(7) needs / too / sensitive / was / to / she / of / busy / the / sensible / to / children / her / be

(8) strong / son / had / his / was / of / disappointment / feeling / would / she / her / as / make / with / way / Hollywood / a / hoped / she / in / left / deception

(9) streets / towns / experimenting / with / keep / them / the / for / are / some / experiencing / after / young / curfews / the / American / off / to / 10

(10) me / publisher / books / had / editor / not / the / sent / ordered / has / I / the / all

score : ... × 10 = ◯

c) Traduisez en anglais.

(1) Combien son mari gagne-t-il par mois ? Je l'ignore totalement.

(2) Hier j'ai écouté une très bonne adaptation d'une nouvelle de Faulkner à la radio.

(3) Elle a passé son examen et a réussi.

(4) On m'a offert une caméra pour mon anniversaire.

(5) Il travaille pour une agence de publicité.

(6) Les grottes préhistoriques de Lascaux sont connues dans le monde entier.

(7) L'industrialisation s'est souvent faite au préjudice de l'environnement et de la santé de la population.

(8) Cendrillon vivait misérablement à l'ombre de ses sœurs qui la rendaient malheureuse.

(9) Il m'a demandé où était la gare du RER la plus proche et à quelle station il devait descendre.

(10) Son nouveau film a reçu des critiques chaleureuses dans le monde cinématographique.

score : ... × 10 = ◯

HANDLE WITH CARE ! 149

d) Traduisez en français.

(1) Why don't you run down to the liquor-store and get a bottle of liqueur for your grand-father.
(2) When she saw him she pretended she didn't know him and ignored him totally.
(3) Her neighbours consider her a rather decent young women, but extremely extravagant.
(4) If we should experience another oil crisis, Western countries might have to face a rise in petrol prices.
(5) Of the two sisters, Mary Ann has the finer figure.
(6) She sent the children to the garden because they were aggravating her.
(7) I've lost the film I bought this morning.
(8) Lots of people are prejudiced against Gypsies.
(9) Because of the economic crisis the manager wasn't able to meet his workers' demands.
(10) "We started quarrelling and then he verbally abused me," she said crying.

score : ... × 10 =

26.
AMÉRICANISMES

a) Remplacez les mots en anglais britannique en italiques par leur équivalent en anglais américain.

It was a fine **(1)** *autumn* afternoon and she had just finished **(2)** *washing up* after lunch, when she decided to go shopping and leave the children in the **(3)** *flat* with the **(4)** *cleaner* for a few hours.

She took the **(5)** *lift* down to the **(6)** *ground-floor* and walked briskly towards her black car which was parked down the street. First she stopped at the **(7)** *petrol-station* to fill it up.

The traffic was very slow because a **(8)** *lorry* was unloading and blocking the traffic. She was lucky enough to find a parking place in the **(9)** *car park* at the rear of the supermaket.

Inside she looked for a **(10)** *trolley* and started filling it with groceries, **(11)** *tins*, frozen food, **(12)** *biscuits*, **(13)** *crisps*, **(14)** *sweets* and **(15)** *beef ribs*. She then edged her way to the **(16)** *cashier* where she had to **(17)** *queue* for a while and walked out. She put everything in the **(18)** *boot* and since it was twenty **(19)** *past* four and had no time to go to the **(20)** *pictures*, she drove back home.

score : ... × 5 = ◯

b) Choisissez parmi les solutions proposées l'équivalent en anglais britannique du mot américain en italiques.

(1) Could you get me the ice-cream out of the *ice-box* **fridge / freezer / cupboard / deep freeze** please.

(2) In this posh neighbourhood, houses are often *burglarized* **broken into / mortgaged / rehabilitated / restored** during the summer.

(3) The exhibition will open next week in Atlanta in a *two-storied* **two-towered / two-gabled / two-floored / two-levelled** pavilion.

(4) After working with a company for a year, you are given a two weeks' *vacation* **demotion / promotion / replacement job / holiday** with pay.

(5) On weekends he will help his wife *set* **dress / lay / clear / remove** the table.

(6) His car was found shortly after it was stolen, but its *fender* **wing / bumper / bonnet / exhaust-pipe** was smashed and its spare tire was missing.

(7) She isn't a born housewife but at least she *vacuums* **waxes / drycleans / dusts / hoovers** the house once in a while.

(8) As she was fumbling in her *purse* **shopping-bag / handbag / knapsack / wallet**, her keys dropped on the (9) *sidewalk* **pavement / floor / roadway / asphalt**.

10 She bought each of the children a pair of expensive *sneakers* **galoshes / trainers / jumpers / loafers**.

score : ... × 10 = ◯

152 AMÉRICANISMES

c) Remettez les éléments en ordre de façon à reconstituer une phrase cohérente. Dans chaque phrase, un élément doit être omis, selon la consigne, le terme en anglais britannique (GB) ou américain (US).

(1) **(US)** States / colour / in / mail-boxes / are / United / what / the / letter-boxes / ?

(2) **(GB)** Madam / engaged / moment / can't / sorry / put / the / line / at / the / busy / through / I / your / is / call

(3) **(US)** beautiful / famous / seen / have / ? / launderette / the / you / film / laundromat / British / called / my

(4) **(US)** sugar-bowl / kitchen / you / cupboard / will / the / find / on / the / in / shelf / closet / the / bottom

(5) **(GB)** successful / car / scene / of / most / takes / the / crowded / place / of / carriage / in / train / a / the / film / a

score : ... × 20 = ◯

d) Remplacez le mot en anglais américain en italiques par son équivalent en anglais britannique.

(1) No wonder she's putting on weight, she eats nothing but hamburgers and *French fries*.

(2) Don't throw your bottles into the *garbage-can*. Save them for recycling.

AMÉRICANISMES 153

- **(3)** Can I borrow your *eraser* please ?
- **(4)** Penn Station is New York City's biggest *railroad* station.
- **(5)** The island of Granada is a paradise for *vacationers*.
- **(6)** In New York the fastest way to get around is to travel by *subway*.
- **(7)** After the demonstration, 65 protesters were shoved into *police wagons* and taken to the nearby police station.
- **(8)** When they went back to the car there was a parking ticket under the *windshield* wiper.
- **(9)** "Hello Operator, I'd like to *make a collect call* to Bridgeport, Connecticut, please".
- **(10)** American *licence plates* sometimes bear their owner's name.

score : ... × 10 =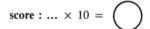

CORRIGÉS

1. L'ARTICLE

A. L'ARTICLE INDÉFINI

a) **(1)** an - **(2)** an - **(3)** an - **(4)** a - **(5)** an - **(6)** an - **(7)** a - **(8)** a - **(9)** a - **(10)** a - **(11)** an - **(12)** a - **(13)** a - **(14)** a - **(15)** an - **(16)** a - **(17)** an - **(18)** a - **(19)** a - **(20)** a.

b) **(1)** an - **(2)** a - **(3)** ∅ - **(4)** a - **(5)** a - **(6)** ∅ - **(7)** ∅ - **(8)** a - **(9)** a - **(10)** a - **(11)** a - **(12)** ∅ - **(13)** a - **(14)** an - **(15)** an - **(16)** an - **(17)** a - **(18)** ∅ - **(19)** a - **(20)** ∅.

B. L'ARTICLE DÉFINI

a) **(1)** ∅ - **(2)** ∅ - **(3)** ∅ - **(4)** ∅ - **(5)** the - **(6)** ∅ - **(7)** ∅ - **(8)** the - **(9)** the - **(10)** ∅ - **(11)** ∅ - **(12)** ∅ - **(13)** the - **(14)** the - **(15)** ∅ - **(16)** the - **(17)** the - **(18)** ∅ - **(19)** the / ∅ - **(20)** ∅.

b) **(1)** ∅ - **(2)** ∅ - **(3)** ∅ - **(4)** ∅ - **(5)** ∅ - **(6)** ∅ - **(7)** the - **(8)** ∅ - **(9)** ∅ - **(10)** ∅ - **(11)** the - **(12)** the - **(13)** the - **(14)** ∅ - **(15)** ∅ - **(16)** ∅ - **(17)** the - **(18)** the - **(19)** the - **(20)** ∅.

C. ARTICLE DÉFINI OU INDÉFINI

a) **(1)** the - **(2)** a - **(3)** a - **(4)** the - **(5)** ∅ - **(6)** a - **(7)** ∅ - **(8)** The - **(9)** ∅ - **(10)** the - **(11)** ∅ - **(12)** the - **(13)** ∅ - **(14)** a - **(15)** the - **(16)** the - **(17)** The - **(18)** ∅ - **(19)** ∅/the - **(20)** The - **(21)** ∅/the - **(22)** The - **(23)** the - **(24)** The - **(25)** ∅.

b) **(1)** a - **(2)** ∅ - **(3)** ∅ - **(4)** ∅ - **(5)** the - **(6)** an - **(7)** a - **(8)** The - **(9)** The - **(10)** ∅ (the) - **(11)** ∅ (the) - **(12)** the - **(13)** ∅ - **(14)** an - **(15)** the - **(16)** ∅ - **(17)** a - **(18)** the - **(19)** ∅ - **(20)** ∅ - **(21)** the - **(22)** the - **(23)** the - **(24)** the - **(25)** ∅.

c) **(1)** The - **(2)** a - **(3)** ∅ - **(4)** a - **(5)** ∅ - **(6)** a - **(7)** ∅ - **(8)** ∅ - **(9)** ∅ - **(10)** the - **(11)** a - **(12)** the - **(13)** the - **(14)** the - **(15)** the - **(16)** a - **(17)** the - **(18)** a - **(19)** ∅ - **(20)** the - **(21)** a - **(22)** the - **(23)** ∅ - **(24)** ∅ - **(25)** ∅.

d) **(1)** Have you got a light ? - **(2)** Brush your teeth every day ! - **(3)** One day you'll understand ! - **(4)** You saved my life ! - **(5)** He shook hands with the President. - **(6)** He is home-sick. - **(7)** Let's go home. - **(8)** There's no hurry, we've got plenty of time. - **(9)** Dinner is ready / Dinner is served ! - **(10)** Fill it/her up, please.

2. LE NOM

A. LE PLURIEL DES NOMS

a) **(1)** brushes - **(2)** boxes - **(3)** benches - **(4)** scarves - **(5)** mice - **(6)** children - **(7)** teeth - **(8)** tooth-fairies - **(9)** volcanoes/volcanos - **(10)** men - **(11)** wives - **(12)** handkerchiefs - **(13)** women - **(14)** machines - **(15)** pennies - **(16)** feet - **(17)** grand-pianos - **(18)** roofs - **(19)** geese - **(20)** lice.

b) **(1)** Waleses - **(2)** Tigers - **(3)** elephants - **(4)** species - **(5)** grown-ups - **(6)** countries - **(7)** equilibrium - **(8)** equality - **(9)** have-nots - **(10)** haves - **(11)** tennis fans - **(12)** ups and downs - **(13)** bases - **(14)** g's - **(15)** Wallets - **(16)** purses - **(17)** thieves - **(18)** cash - **(19)** advice - **(20)** University people - **(21)** MP's / MPs - **(22)** sessions - **(23)** Fruit - **(24)** Women-drivers - **(25)** counterparts - **(26)** passers-by - **(27)** beliefs - **(28)** pence - **(29)** brothers-in-law - **(30)** savings-banks.

B. LES SUFFIXES

a) **(1)** novelist - **(2)** cleverness - **(3)** usherette - **(4)** mouthful - **(5)** cooker - **(6)** neighbourhood - **(7)** employment - **(8)** employee - **(9)** quotation - **(10)** capitalism.

b) **(1)** criticism - **(2)** misery - **(3)** efficiency - **(4)** denial - **(5)** poverty - **(6)** wisdom - **(7)** lengths - **(8)** waiter - **(9)** waitress - **(10)** jewellery (GB)/jewelry (US).

c) **(1)** maturity - **(2)** starvation - **(3)** manhood - **(4)** pilgrimage - **(5)** drunkenness - **(6)** illiteracy - **(7)**

mankind - **(8)** membership - **(9)** expectation - **(10)** weight.

C. LES NOMS COMPOSÉS

a) **(1)** customs-officer - **(2)** sleeping-pill - **(3)** drinking-water - **(4)** dish-washer - **(5)** video (cassette) recorder - **(6)** tax-collector - **(7)** weather-report - **(8)** camping-ground (site) - **(9)** right-winger - **(10)** microwave.

b) **(1)** drop-out - **(2)** good-for-nothing - **(3)** footsteps - **(4)** the man-in-the-street - **(5)** bath-robe - **(6)** stairway/staircase - **(7)** step-mother - **(8)** piggy-banks - **(9)** daydreams - **(10)** pipe-dreams.

D. LES NOMS DE NATIONALITÉ

a) **(1)** The British - **(2)** The Portuguese - **(3)** The Danes - **(4)** Puerto-Ricans - **(5)** Mexicans - **(6)** The Greeks - **(7)** Germans - **(8)** Vietnamese - **(9)** Cambodians - **(10)** Israelis.

b) **(1)** Pole - **(2)** Briton / Britisher (péjoratif) - **(3)** Scot - **(4)** Spaniard - **(5)** Dutchman - **(6)** Finns - **(7)** Swedes - **(8)** Japanese - **(9)** Norwegians - **(10)** Iraqi.

3. LA POSSESSION

a) (1) motorist's - (2) women's rights - (3) The Moscow Mc Donald's - (4) a day's wages - (5) Andy's and Jesse's - (6) S. Lewis's life - (7) his uncle's grocer's shop - (8) the United States constitution - (9) this man's - (10) World War II uniform.

b) (1) Society's institutions and values - (2) hour's delay - (3) 16-and-17-year-olds - (4) one's - (5) to hers - (6) the Osbornes' - (7) the man-in-the-street - (8) at arm's length - (9) last week's *Financial Times* - (10) the Wright brothers' flight - (11) For God's sake - (12) her mother's - (13) Britain's - (14) day's work / day's pay - (15) deer's antlers - (16) his wife's - (17) his parents' reaction - (18) the world's 1st airline - (19) the baker's shop - (20) the nation's capital.

4. L'ADJECTIF

A. LA PLACE DE L'ADJECTIF

(1) He lived in a spacious, scantily furnished five-room apartment in a restored New England house. - (2) He is a tall, balding, middle-aged man with worn, angular features. - (3) He presented the headmaster with a dirty, yellowed, gnarled hand to shake. - (4) Every single working day in the past ten years, he has never left his office before eight. - (5) Ellis Island's long-slung main building of warm red brick and large paned-windows has a surprisingly welcoming air today.

B. LES DEGRÉS DE COMPARAISON

a) (1) thinner - (2) largest - (3) heavier - (4) the most radical - (5) the most polluted - (6) the least habitable - (7) greater and greater - (8) the worst - (9) better - (10) the best.

b) (1) higher - (2) less affluent - (3) (the) most - (4) the toughest - (5) (the) fiercest - (6) (the) hardest - (7) most - (8) latest - (9) finest - (10) as well-written as.

c) (1) The more perfect the negative is, the better the print will be. - (2) There were fewer mistakes in your essay this time than last time. - (3) Japanese video recorders are cheaper (less expensive) than German ones. - (4) His poetry is worse than (not as good as) his short-stories. - (5) I can't speak Italian as well as I can understand it.

C. LES ADJECTIFS COMPOSÉS

a) **(1)** a red-haired little girl - **(2)** an upper-class family - **(3)** a self-centered nation - **(4)** 19,321-feet high Kilimanjaro - **(5)** a self-respecting budding poet - **(6)** a South African-born singer - **(7)** a three-decade exile - **(8)** navy-blue - **(9)** colour-blind - **(10)** a couldn't-care-less attitude.

b) **(1)** high-speed - **(2)** long-standing - **(3)** double-deckers - **(4)** time-honoured - **(5)** X-rated - **(6)** open-heart - **(7)** bad-tempered - **(8)** red-handed - **(9)** second-hand - **(10)** made-to-measure.

D. LES ADJECTIFS DE NATIONALITÉ

(1) Chinese - **(2)** Swiss - **(3)** Soviet - **(4)** Finnish - **(5)** Hungarian - **(6)** Irish - **(7)** Belgian - **(8)** Danish - **(9)** Pakistani - **(10)** Welsh.

E. LES PRÉFIXES

(1) impolite - **(2)** unpleasant - **(3)** dissatisfied - **(4)** unbalanced - **(5)** incapable - **(6)** impartial - **(7)** unbelievable - **(8)** impatient - **(9)** discontented - **(10)** uncomfortable - **(11)** inexpensive - **(12)** unlucky - **(13)** disagreeable - **(14)** dishonest - **(15)** inconvenient - **(16)** unrealistic - **(17)** unfair - **(18)** displeased - **(19)** unequal - **(20)** dishonourable.

F. TEST RÉCAPITULATIF

(1) The sooner, the better - **(2)** the fancier one - **(3)** millions of - **(4)** the supernatural / the dark - **(5)** the eldest - **(6)** Italians - **(7)** his best - **(8)** 600 million - **(9)** no fewer than - **(10)** for the better - **(11)** the homeless - **(12)** 48 years old - **(13)** thousand / hundreds of thousands - **(14)** as - **(15)** the longer / the wiser - **(16)** least - **(17)** all the more devastating as - **(18)** none the worse for it - **(19)** the upper hand - **(20)** young people.

5. LE PRONOM

A. PRONOMS RÉFLÉCHIS ET PRONOMS RÉCIPROQUES

(1) yourselves - (2) the two of us - (3) ∅ - (4) themselves - (5) ∅ - (6) each other's - (7) ∅ - (8) each other - (9) each other - (10) themselves - (11) of my own - (12) all by herself - (13) each other - (14) herself - (15) itself - (16) ∅/myself - (17) herself - (18) oneself - (19) ∅ - (20) for yourself.

B. LES PRONOMS RELATIFS

a) (1) who(m) - (2) what - (3) which - (4) whose - (5) who - (6) whose - (7) which - (8) What - (9) whose / the editor of which - (10) who.

b) (1) what - (2) when - (3) whom - (4) what - (5) why - (6) that - (7) of whom - (8) that - (9) that/which - (10) of which - (11) whom - (12) which - (13) What - (14) That - (15) which - (16) whose - (17) whomever - (18) that - (19) What with - (20) that.

c) (1) That's what I need. - (2) I don't know the conductor you're talking about / about whom you're talking / whom you're talking about. - (3) Don't ask questions the answers to which are obvious. - (4) His recovery depends on how he will take to the new antibiotic. - (5) I don't like the way he looks at me. - (6) Why don't you go and see Dr Eliot whose surgery is 5 minutes away from your house. - (7) He passed his exam, which he is very proud of. - (8) Do what I tell you. - (9) She used to say that her son would end up being good for nothing, which turned out to be true. - **(10)** He's a real gem ! He fixes everything that doesn't work in the house.

6. LES QUANTIFIEURS

a) **(1)** any - **(2)** a - **(3)** some - **(4)** no - **(5)** some - **(6)** any - **(7)** nobody/noone - **(8)** no - **(9)** anything - **(10)** a - **(11)** no - **(12)** anywhere - **(13)** some - **(14)** a - **(15)** Anyone - **(16)** no - **(17)** any - **(18)** anything - **(19)** any - **(20)** anything - **(21)** any - **(22)** anyone/anybody - **(23)** Somebody/Someone - **(24)** anywhere - **(25)** Nobody/Noone.

b) **(1)** any / much / enough - **(2)** so much - **(3)** a few / some - **(4)** any - **(5)** few / no - **(6)** some / a few - **(7)** little - **(8)** some - **(9)** too much - **(10)** much - **(11)** any - **(12)** enough - **(13)** much - **(14)** many / some - **(15)** no / little - **(16)** some - **(17)** many - **(18)** no - **(19)** some - **(20)** too many - **(21)** some / all / much - **(22)** many - **(23)** much - **(24)** enough - **(25)** no, no, no, no.

N.B. Dans tous les cas, "many" et "much" peuvent être remplacés par "a lot of", "lots of".

c) **(1)** each - **(2)** several - **(3)** everyone / everybody - **(4)** the whole - **(5)** all / all - **(6)** either - **(7)** every - **(8)** All - **(9)** most - **(10)** both - **(11)** All - **(12)** Neither ... nor - **(13)** both her - **(14)** everything - **(15)** several - **(16)** neither of them - **(17)** each - **(18)** the whole - **(19)** either... or - **(20)** most.

d) **(1)** anything - **(2)** noone - **(3)** anywhere - **(4)** one - **(5)** as many as - **(6)** another - **(7)** somebody else's / everybody's - **(8)** None - **(9)** ones - **(10)** any such - **(11)** any too - **(12)** anything other - **(13)** anyone - **(14)** neither of them / anything - **(15)** fewer and fewer - **(16)** one - **(17)** none - **(18)** anything - **(19)** other - **(20)** all too.

7. L'ADVERBE

a) **(1)** She had seen her before, but didn't really remember her. - **(2)** I am altogether pleased with my new car. - **(3-4-5-6)** He is always in a hurry ; consequently he rarely does anything well. - **(7)** Some people still believe that men and women have an unequal number of ribs. - **(8)** There won't be enough room / room enough in the boot for all that luggage. - **(9-10-11)** Education was still quite elitist then. - **(12)** Among other things he had also been a car salesman. - **(13-14)** He does not usually / Usually he does not / He usually does not smoke very much. - **(15-16-17)** Contrary to popular belief, still very few people speak English fluently nowadays. - **(18)** He always brings her a dozen roses on Mother's day. - **(19)** She ordered a drink from the waiter, but as he didn't come quickly enough, she became annoyed. - **(20)** I very much need a new tennis racket.

b) **(1)** We will be on holiday almost any day now. - **(2)** She talked rather incessantly, but intelligently nevertheless. - **(3)** I stopped reading books completely because they invariably made me think too much. - **(4)** We usually have (Usually we have) club meetings only once a week. - **(5)** It is getting really warm out already (It is already getting really warm out) ; you had better be off right away.

c) **(1)** Never would he repeat my secret to anyone. - **(2)** Hardly does she ever feed them greens. - **(3)** Under no circumstances will I tell you where my money is hidden. - **(4)** Seldom did he socialize with the natives. - **(5)** Up you go now, it's time for bed. - **(6)** Never in my life have I met anyone as conceited as this man. - **(7)** Not once has he told me he loved me in ten years of living together. - **(8)** Hardly had two months gone by when her car broke down. - **(9)** Nowhere in his autobiography does he refer to his children by his first marriage. - **(10)** Off they went loaded down with their camping-car.

d) **(1)** hardly - **(2)** yet - **(3)** yet - **(4)** ever - **(5)** ever - **(6)** still - **(7)** far - **(8)** again - **(9)** before - **(10)** ever - **(11)** ever - **(12)** still - **(13)** already / not yet - **(14)** ever - **(15)** hardly ever - **(16)** therefore - **(17)** here - **(18)** ever again - **(19)** either - **(20)** hardly any.

8. INFINITIF ET GÉRONDIF

a) (1) Stealing - (2) to tell - (3) grumbling - (4) complaining - (5) think - (6) feeling - (7) learning - (8) have - (9) making - (10) have.

b) (1) hearing - (2) to get - (3) to bring - (4) getting - (5) seeing - (6) replacing - (7) proliferating - (8) to go - (9) to be - (10) admiring.

c) (1) paying - (2) grow - (3) stay / spend - (4) showing up / telling - (5) sending - (6) for him to have - (7) to having seen - (8) getting - (9) its being noticed - (10) cook.

d) (1) to do - (2) telling - (3) telling / beating - (4) to grow up thinking - (5) drive - (6) to denounce - (7) of being/playing - (8) to get rid of - (9) to pick - (10) for hitting - (11) to answer - (12) running - (13) denying - (14) wait and see - (15) to re-emphasize - (16) to believe - (17) to make / feel - (18) drinking / talking - (19) to drip - (20) by throwing / limiting.

e) (1) He plans to go mountaineering in New Zealand. - (2) I can't stand your answering your mother back. - (3) He eventually managed to find his way home. - (4) I've given up reading novels... - (5) I can't afford to lose money in that deal. - (6) I don't mind your inviting your friends for the weekend. - (7) What about taking the children to the circus ? - (8) Mother insists on our going to the dentist twice a year. - (9) She is certain to be a great success. - (10) She accused him of neglecting all his duties.

f) **(1)** coming to grips - **(2)** denying - **(3)** becoming - **(4)** hearing - **(5)** downplaying - **(6)** reporting - **(7)** to become - **(8)** to provoke - **(9)** (to) be perceived - **(10)** to live - **(11)** to do - **(12)** to remember - **(13)** being - **(14)** not buying - **(15)** buying - **(16)** buy - **(17)** wanting - **(18)** to buy - **(19)** to retain - **(20)** to get used to - **(21)** seeing - **(22)** take - **(23)** to impose - **(24)** double - **(25)** to become.

g) **(1)** On entering the kitchen I smelt (smelled) gas. - **(2)** There's no starting my car, it's no use flooding the engine. - **(3)** Parents used to be able to punish their children by locking them up in their rooms. - **(4)** Go wash your hands before coming to dinner. - **(5)** I'm looking forward to hearing from you soon. - **(6)** Many people feel safer carrying a gun. - **(7)** She burnt (burned) herself while taking the chicken out of the oven. - **(8)** No one can get used to being discriminated against. - **(9)** He succeeded in overcoming his fear of diving. - **(10)** As a child, I was discouraged from writing poetry.

9. LE PRÉSENT

a) **(1)** is talking about - **(2)** demands - **(3)** grows - **(4)** requires - **(5)** are showing - **(6)** are you feeling - **(7)** don't feel - **(8)** is sitting - **(9)** do we do - **(10)** is stuffing - **(11)** touches - **(12)** bear - **(3)** is ironing - **(14)** are looking for - **(15)** are starting - **(16)** is becoming - **(17)** take - **(18)** wake up - **(19)** am forever forgetting - **(20)** proves - **(21)** is coming back / comes back - **(22)** are you being / are you - **(23)** do you hear - **(24)** aren't listening - **(25)** go.

b) **(1)** donate - **(2)** meet - **(3)** are getting - **(4)** is trying/are trying - **(5)** goes - **(6)** eats - **(7)** are seeing - **(8)** die - **(9)** are spending - **(10)** am seeing - **(11)** see - **(12)** touches - **(13)** fall - **(14)** is expecting - **(15)** Are you thinking - **(16)** thinks - **(17)** are lacking - **(18)** stands up - **(19)** walks - **(20)** are being - **(21)** is having - **(22)** have - **(23)** are taking - **(24)** are really looking - **(25)** am looking/look (more formal).

10. LES TEMPS DU PASSÉ

a) **(1)** were awaiting - **(2)** was changing - **(3)** took - **(4)** blew - **(5)** was tending - **(6)** were flying - **(7)** crashed - **(8)** was snowing - **(9)** passed away - **(10)** checked out - **(11)** did not wake me up - **(12)** was reading - **(13)** were still dancing - **(14)** owned - **(15)** passed by - **(16)** was being played - **(17)** were you doing - **(18)** was working - **(19)** noticed - **(20)** was being watched.

b) **(1)** have seen - **(2)** has given - **(3)** had to - **(4)** have left - **(5)** were unemployed - **(6)** wrote - **(7)** have gone - **(8)** called on - **(9)** was born - **(10)** was educated - **(11)** has published - **(12)** has replaced - **(13)** visited - **(14)** have you been - **(15)** visited - **(16)** couldn't - **(17)** was - **(18)** has lost / lost - **(19)** has been looking for - **(20)** hasn't found.

c) **(1)** was - **(2)** has been working - **(3)** has been publishing - **(4)** has been severely curtailed - **(5)** were imported - **(6)** has been interested in - **(7)** led - **(8)** made - **(9)** have been waiting - **(10)** has mushroomed.

d) **(1)** for 3 weeks - **(2)** A week ago - **(3)** since 1971 - **(4)** 10 days ago - **(5)** since he bought his Austin - **(6)** for ages - **(7)** 2 months ago - **(8)** since the children left - **(9)** for years - **(10)** since he stopped smoking.

e) **(1)** His play has been on Broadway for two years. - **(2)** Ever since he married her he has been complaining about the bills she has run up. - **(3)** The books he has written since he has moved abroad are supposed to be excellent. - **(4)** It is three years since the last tornado blew over the West Indies. - **(5)** As recently as two years ago bungee-jumping was little known except to a few sky-divers or mountain-climbers.

f) **(1)** c - **(2)** a - **(3)** e - **(4)** d - **(5)** b.

g) **(1)** was born - **(2)** have you been writing - **(3)** has known - **(4)** had nursed - **(5)** turned down - **(6)** had promised - **(7)** have tried / have met - **(8)** in - **(9)** How long - **(10)** had dared - **(11)** a week ago - **(12)** had deliberated - **(13)** was Ellis Island turned into - **(14)** began - **(15)** bought - **(16)** Since when - **(17)** started - **(18)** has helped - **(19)** did find - **(20)** has gained - **(21)** quilted 50 years ago - **(22)** has become - **(23)** rented - **(24)** has changed / visited - **(25)** is it since.

11. LE FUTUR

(1) will be - **(2)** I'm going to call / I'll do - **(3)** 4 solutions justes - **(4)** will be wondering - **(5)** is yet to come - **(6)** was about to - **(7)** is going to be - **(8)** will be - **(9)** are planning / is going to be - **(10)** wouldn't open - **(11)** will pay - **(12)** leaves - **(13)** shall continue - **(14)** are bound to be - **(15)** will revert - **(16)** was expecting - **(17)** was to take - **(18)** have slept - **(19)** will have been reached - **(20)** was to have been - **(21)** marry - **(22)** will be turning - **(23)** will have spent - **(24)** receives - **(25)** will be.

12. LE CONDITIONNEL

a) (1) Would - (2) would - (3) should - (4) would - (5) Shouldn't / Should - (6) shouldn't - (7) should - (8) would - (9) would not - (10) should - (11) should not - (12) Would - (13) should not - (14) would - (15) should - (16) would - (17) would - (18) Would - (19) should - (20) should.

b) (1) would have caught - (2) would see - (3) could he want - (4) would not have finished - (5) would not have considered / would not consider (idée de modalité) - (6) Would you be interested in - (7) would never have noticed - (8) would not want - (9) wouldn't have arrested - (10) would never have expected.

c) (1) would have burst - (2) would be - (3) might need - (4) would have to - (5) would you - (6) would have left - (7) would have been able to - (8) could you do - (9) want - (10) should need - (11) would have been - (12) could do - (13) live - (14) should - (15) would come - (16) 4 solutions justes - (17) couldn't possibly have done - (18) has - (19) won't - (20) should forget.

13. LES AUXILIAIRES MODAUX

A. FORMES SIMPLES

a) (i) **(1)** may - **(2)** should - **(3)** could - **(4)** mustn't - **(5)** can.
   (ii) **(6)** can't - **(7)** needn't - **(8)** could - **(9)** must - **(10)** might.

b) **(1)** should - **(2)** Shall - **(3)** should - **(4)** won't - **(5)** Would - **(6)** should - **(7)** will - **(8)** shall - **(9)** Would - **(10)** would.

B. FORMES COMPOSÉES ET ÉQUIVALENTS

a) **(1)** wouldn't have been allowed - **(2)** should never have resorted - **(3)** ought not to - **(4)** had to - **(5)** should be allowed to - **(6)** wouldn't - **(7)** must have been - **(8)** shouldn't be used - **(9)** wouldn't have to - **(10)** can't be - **(11)** might have been - **(12)** can't be / might be able to - **(13)** needn't - **(14)** will be able to - **(15)** must have been - **(16)** won't - **(17)** can't have lost - **(18)** will - **(19)** may / have had to close - **(20)** Should people be allowed - **(21)** would have adopted - **(22)** haven't to - **(23)** might not - **(24)** could have - **(25)** ought.

b) **(1)** His parents must have helped him. - **(2)** Lots of women today can't cook. - **(3)** They might take you in. - **(4)** He can't have bought a Japanese car. - **(5)** You should / ought to reserve your seats. - **(6)** You needn't / don't have to hoover the floor every day. - **(7)** They had to remodel their house. - **(8)** Your flat may be burgled. - **(9)** It mustn't go any further. - **(10)** You must carry traveler's checks.

176 LES AUXILIAIRES MODAUX

c) (1) When she took the train to Eton, she was not allowed to take her dog. - **(2)** Being able to drive a car in America is a mark of being an adult. - **(3)** I'm sorry to have to tell you that you're not eligible. - **(4)** She assured me I didn't have to drink my cocktail if I didn't like it. - **(5)** I'd rather park in a car-park. - **(6)** He was to outlive his wife by 10 years. - **(7)** She still hasn't been able to make him understand her point of view. - **(8)** I saved time, I didn't have to look up her number. — **(9)** You shouldn't / you'd better not / you ought not to flaunt your wealth. - **(10)** He can't be a terrorist.

C. TESTS RÉCAPITULATIFS

a) (1) might - **(2)** should be hijacked - **(3)** Should - **(4)** may - **(5)** shouldn't be - **(6)** should - **(7)** may be - **(8)** should - **(9)** I could get over - **(10)** she should call.

b) (1) They shouldn't be long. - **(2)** She must have forgotten to add salt. - **(3)** Everybody must (has to) die. - **(4)** You should have written your address on the back of the envelope. - **(5)** Shall I wrap it up for you, Madam ? - **(6)** He's 18. He's to take his first driving-lesson tomorrow. - **(7)** He's a self-made man. He owes nothing to his parents. - **(8)** You mustn't beat a child. - **(9)** Many accidents are due to (are caused by) drunken drivers. - **(10)** Sure enough ! He was bound to cut himself with that knife.

14. LES VERBES COMPOSÉS

a) (1) Can you look up her telephone number / Can you look her telephone number up - (2) Should a spy give away any information / give any information away - (3) There's no waking him up - (4) We'll have to close down two of our branches / We'll have to close two of our branches down - (5) You should call them up - (6) He shaved them off - (7) He's just run across a friend - (8) I might drop in on her - (9) We must work something out / work out something - (10) We'll ever run out of oil.

b) (1) to look into - (2) give up - (3) call on - (4) find out - (5) get off - (6) made up - (7) were broken into - (8) wash away - (9) brought up - (10) look on.

c) (1) make out - (2) stand for - (3) got your doctorate dissertation over with - (4) take over from - (5) fell for - (6) ran into - (7) waited on - (8) going on - (9) takes after - (10) live through.

d) (1) shouldn't have refused - (2) stalled - (3) must have informed on - (4) would become involved - (5) to decide not to do it - (6) was announced - (7) to put the receiver back on the hook - (8) doesn't save - (9) to encounter - (10) to reduce.

e) (1) up - (2) over - (3) out - (4) off - (5) out - (6) on - (7) up with - (8) along - (9) up with - (10) out.

f) (1) Marilyn - (2) Emily - (3) Martha - (4) Bob - (5) Christine - (6) Sam - (7) Rose - (8) Dora - (9) the union leader - (10) Harry.

15. LES REPRISES VERBALES

A. LES "QUESTION-TAGS"

a) **(1)** won't he ? - **(2)** have you ? - **(3)** aren't they ? - **(4)** could he ? - **(5)** mustn't you ? - **(6)** would he ? **(7)** doesn't she ? **(8)** can she ? - **(9)** was there ? - **(10)** didn't they ?

b) **(1)** didn't she ? - **(2)** shall we ? - **(3)** would he ? - **(4)** need you ? - **(5)** isn't it ? - **(6)** shouldn't they ? - **(7)** isn't it ? - **(8)** is it ? - **(9)** will you ? - **(10)** had you ? - **(11)** hasn't it ? - **(12)** did they ? - **(13)** didn't they ? - **(14)** aren't we ? - **(15)** haven't you ? - **(16)** is there ? **(17)** didn't you ? - **(18)** did she ? - **(19)** will you ? - **(20)** didn't he ? - **(21)** aren't I ? - **(22)** will it ? - **(23)** hadn't she ? - **(24)** do they ? - **(25)** doesn't he ?

B. LES "TAGS" DE RÉPONSE

a) **(1)** "Does he ?" - **(2)** but your mother will. - **(3)** "So it is." - **(4)** "Oh, you can't, can't you ?" - **(5)** but many people do. - **(6)** was he ? - **(7)** "So do Japanese firms." - **(8)** but mine don't. - **(9)** "Neither has anybody else." - **(10)** "So is French cooking."

b) **(1)** "So do lots of people." - **(2)** but German shepherds aren't. - **(3)** "Oh they are, are they ?" - **(4)** "So he did." - **(5)** but my wife does. - **(6)** neither can they. - **(7)** so do I. - **(8)** but lots of women wouldn't. - **(9)** "Did you ?" - **(10)** nor did his cats.

LES REPRISES VERBALES

c) **(1)** but she must. - **(2)** "So he did." - **(3)** everybody does. - **(4)** please have. - **(5)** "Oh, he doesn't ?" - **(6)** so did I. - **(7)** but his brother won't. - **(8)** pas d'intrus - **(9)** but Charles wouldn't. - **(10)** "Yes, we shall."

16. LES QUESTIONS

a) **(1)** Who - **(2)** Whose - **(3)** How far - **(4)** How long - **(5)** How many - **(6)** Who(m) - **(7)** Which - **(8)** What colour - **(9)** Where - **(10)** Why.

b) **(1)** How can he get there ? - **(2)** When is the film showing ? - **(3)** Why was the traffic diverted ? - **(4)** Who is building the Chunnel ? - **(5)** How much does she make a year ? - **(6)** How long ago was it abolished ? - **(7)** Where were there lots of tourists last year ? - **(8)** Who(m) would they like to go to Disneyland with ? - **(9)** How long did she rule (for) ? - **(10)** Who was he arrested by ?

c) **(1)** Where did they leave from ? - **(2)** Who does he take after ? - **(3)** What did he signal him to do ? - **(4)** Who was sent to the state prison ? - **(5)** Who(m) should he invite to the theatre ? - **(6)** What would you like to borrow a jack for ? - **(7)** Which congressman would he rather have voted for ? - **(8)** Whose car is parked on the wrong side of the street ? - **(9)** What time did they have to get up ? - **(10)** What does he usually spend his holidays doing ? / How does he usually spend his holidays ? - **(11)** How high is Mount Everest ? - **(12)** Whose house will they be spending the night at ? - **(13)** Where did they use to spend Christmas ? - **(14)** How many times have I already told you to stop shouting ? - **(15)** How long has this been going on ? - **(16)** How often should you feed the dog ? - **(17)** How many million pets are there in Great Britain ? - **(18)** Since when have you been sunbathing ? - **(19)** What did he apologize for ? - **(20)** How big is your new apartment ?

LES QUESTIONS

d) (1) What's his name ? - **(2)** How do you spell his last name ? - **(3)** How old is he ? - **(4)** When and where was he born ? - **(5)** What's his address ? - **(6)** What's his marital status ? - **(7)** How tall is he ? - **(8)** How much does he weigh ? - **(9)** What size shoe does he take ? (GB) What size shoe does he wear ? / What size shoe is he (US) ? - **(10)** What does he look like ?

e) (1) What's on TV ? - **(2)** What will you have ? / What are you having ? / May (can) I take your order (US) ? - **(3)** What's the weather like ? - **(4)** What's for dinner / lunch ? - **(5)** How much did you pay for it ? / How much was it ? / How much did it cost ? - **(6)** Shall we have a drink ? - **(7)** What's the English for "panda" ? / What do you call a "panda" in English ? - **(8)** Who gave you that ring ? - **(9)** What is it for ? - **(10)** Have you ever been away from home ?

17. LES STRUCTURES VERBALES

A. LES CAUSATIFS : "FAIRE FAIRE"

a) **(1)** made - **(2)** won't get - **(3)** will have - **(4)** made - **(5)** were often made - **(6)** to have - **(7)** making - **(8)** Did I make/Have I made - **(9)** was made - **(10)** to get.

b) **(1)** The Principal showed the boarders around the school. - **(2)** Why did you frighten them ? - **(3)** "Mr Lennox is here to see you (would like to see you) sir". "Let him in". - **(4)** You mustn't keep ladies waiting. - **(5)** Have you warmed up the stew ? - **(6)** Show him/her your new skateboard. - **(7)** She had to call for the doctor in the middle of the night. - **(8)** You dropped your glove. - **(9)** Let us know it you want us to meet you at the station. - **(10)** His driver's licence was suspended for speeding.

c) **(1)** The customs-officer made him open / had him open (US) his suitcase. - **(2)** He wants to have his next-door neighbour arrested for indecent exposure. - **(3)** No matter how hard I tried I couldn't get him to stop taking sleeping pills. - **(4)** As he didn't pay his bills, he had his phone disconnected. - **(5)** The Americans made the Chinese build / had the Chinese build (US) the Union Pacific Railway. - **(6)** They must have their flat painted by the end of the week. - **(7)** Being an actress, she could make herself cry anytime she wanted. - **(8)** Every week, she has her hair done at the most expensive hairdresser's. - **(9)** Muslims make everybody take their shoes off when entering a mosque. - **(10)** She wants to have her tooth pulled out by the best oral surgeon.

LES STRUCTURES VERBALES

B. LA PROPOSITION INFINITIVE

a) **(1)** She doesn't expect them to arrive before 8 : 00. - **(2)** Mum always wants him to help her to do the washing-up. - **(3)** She told her to finish her homework. - **(4)** The policeman ordered them to move back. - **(5)** He advised me not to overwork myself. - **(6)** I sincerely wish her to be happy. - **(7)** Roy asked us to stop fighting and make up. - **(8)** They'd prefer him not to stay at his friend's house overnight. - **(9)** It won't be necessary for us to change trains. **(10)** He doesn't want them to be known.

b) **(1)** "Here is some money for the fair, Steve, but I don't want you to go into the bumper-cars." - **(2)** It is time for the government to find a solution to the problem of drugs. - **(3)** The adman wishes the viewers to associate the atmosphere of refinement and luxury of this southern plantation with the product. - **(4)** The sun is too hot today for me to stay on the beach. - **(5)** It will be necessary for you to check her address in the telephone book. - **(6)** They are lending their son money for him to pay for his tuition and fees. - **(7)** He is open-handed enough for everybody to like him. - **(8)** We'll have a contract ready for you to sign in a week. - **(9)** Your car is too small for us to all fit in. - **(10)** If his son is in trouble, it is natural for him to be upset.

C. STRUCTURES IDIOMATIQUES AVEC INVERSION

(1) Should you be interested in further information about our product, please contact our relations department. - **(2)** No matter how hard he worked, his wife always earned more money than he did. - **(3)** Had I paid more attention to detail as I was reading, I would have guessed who the murderer was. - **(4)** Try as he may, sleep would not come. - **(5)** Were my grandparents alive, what would they make of the world today ? - **(6)** Smart as she was, she could not find a solution to her problem. - **(7)** Little did they know when they defected how hard their new life would be. - **(8)** The higher the standard of living people enjoy, the more difficult they are to please. - **(9)** Come what may, I will never abandon my aged parents. - **(10)** No sooner had the robbers started working on the safe combination than the alarm-system rang.

D. TESTS RÉCAPITULATIFS

a) (1) go out - **(2)** get dressed up - **(3)** leave - **(4)** should be / are - **(5)** to be checked out - **(6)** hadn't been erased - **(7)** to change - **(8)** spending - **(9)** to forward - **(10)** Should you need.

b) (1) b - **(2)** e - **(3)** a - **(4)** d - **(5)** c.

c) (1) d - **(2)** b - **(3)** a - **(4)** e - **(5)** c.

d) (1) Let's - **(2)** I don't want - **(3)** He'll get him - **(4)** She would enjoy - **(5)** I expected.

e) (1) She should have checked the stove / she had turned off the gas before she left the house / leaving the house. - **(2)** They were mugged by a young drug-addict. - **(3)** I couldn't make him / her tell the truth. - **(4)** He had them saved for you. - **(5)** I wish it were already tomorrow evening. - **(6)** Jeremy, I wish you would leave your brother alone. - **(7)** He had rather you didn't ask him any questions about his whereabouts yesterday. - **(8)** I'd rather not see his reaction when he finds out that we own 4 cars. - **(9)** You can't really expect your boss to give you more than a three-week leave of absence holiday. - **(10)** She was looking forward to her husband('s) retiring so that they could travel.

18. L'EXCLAMATION

a) **(1)** How - **(2)** Such an - **(3)** What a - **(4)** What - **(5)** How - **(6)** Such a - **(7)** How - **(8)** What a - **(9)** Such a - **(10)** How.

b) **(1)** What a romantic turn of mind you've got ! - **(2)** How clever of you it was ! - **(3)** He is such a good-looking fellow ! - **(4)** What an ordeal (it was) ! - **(6)** How totally inadequate you make me feel ! - **(7)** What a delicious meal (it was) ! - **(8)** How nice it was to see you again ! - **(9)** What a car ! - **(10)** How very stupidly he acted !

19. PASSIF

a) **(1)** was torn - **(2)** will be done - **(3)** have just been told - **(4)** is still being serviced - **(5)** Should boys and girls be brought up the same way ? - **(6)** had been locked up - **(7)** must have been taken - **(8)** are now requested - **(9)** Are you being attended to ? - **(10)** used to be denied.

b) **(1)** Why weren't those children taught good manners ? - **(2)** Your luggage will be taken care of by the porter. - **(3)** I had been told only part of the truth. - **(4)** Cholera and typhoid are contracted by drinking infected water. - **(5)** All the slums in this area are bound to be torn down by the government one day. - **(6)** The mail has already been collected by the postman. - **(7)** A film about the Sahara is being shot. - **(8)** My mail will be forwarded to me. - **(9)** The workers should be talked into going back to work. - **(10)** Was he told to come back later by the secretary ?

c) **(1)** His business was taken over by his son. - **(2)** His book will be published next month. - **(3)** He was refused entry into the Opera House. - **(4)** He was told not to make a rude remark. - **(5)** She was made to slow down on entering the village. - **(6)** Her husband may be asked to testify in her favour. - **(7)** It was said on the radio that the weather would be cold and rainy tomorrow. - **(8)** Washington is regarded as the greatest of all presidents. - **(9)** Could he be made to confess his crimes ? - **(10)** Were any of the demonstrators arrested by the police ? - **(11)** He is assumed to have worked for the CIA. - **(12)** Pollution is supposed to be reduced drastically by the year 2000. - **(13)** Penguins are relatively friendly animals that can be approached easily.

- **(14)** Money is thought to be the root of all evil. - **(15)** A dam to generate electricity is being built on the Danube. - **(16)** Patrons are often provided with doggie-bags in American restaurants. - **(17)** Nobody likes to be bossed around. - **(18)** He was awarded the Nobel Prize for physics. - **(19)** The extent of the damage won't be known until the flood has receded. - **(20)** She is thought to be a drug-addict.

d) **(1)** was killed - **(2)** are frowned upon - **(3)** are wanted - **(4)** is said to be - **(5)** is thought to have been educated - **(6)** have been heard to quarrel - **(7)** are told - **(8)** are made to work - **(9)** are told - **(10)** to be done with her.

20. LE DISCOURS INDIRECT

a) She said (1) she really enjoyed herself a lot
(2) whenever she went skating. - She remarked (3) that
she had met her husband while running the New York
Marathon. - He inquired (4) what on earth we were / I
was doing there, (5) and what we were / I was up to. -
He asked (6) Eva if she could do him a favour. - They
told her (7) they were afraid (8) they would have to be
going, (9) it was late. - He ordered his secretary (10) to
cancel all his appointments for the afternoon (11) and
not to disturb him for the next 30 minutes. - He told me
(12) that as soon as he was granted his fellowship,
(13) he would start working on his Ph. D. dissertation. -
They asked us (14) if we intended to do some
sightseeing (15) when we were in Canada. - He
remarked (16) it was the easiest thing in the world to
give up smoking, (17) he had done it a hundred times. -
He said (18) it was an emergency, (19) I / we / they
had to come right away. She asked (20) how long I
would be teaching in South Carolina.

b) The gardener told the children that they weren't allowed
to / they weren't to pick flowers in public parks. - He
said (3) he really didn't know (2) whether he should
wait for a taxi or take the bus. - (4) They told the clerk
at the desk (4) not to worry, (5) they would find their
way... - He suggested (6) we should have a look at their
rose garden. - He said (7) that it was many years
(8) since we had met (9) and how time flies. He asked
(10) if I remembered (11) the first time he had seen me.
- She informed them (12) that she might be going...,
(13) and if she did, (14) she wouldn't be back until the

following week. - He asked her **(15)** whether she would be able to make it to their party the following day. - She told me **(16)** he had a heart condition, **(17)** and he knew **(18)** something might happen to him. **(19)** All these months he had been living under a death sentence and failing to take any of the precautions **(20)** that might have commuted it.

c) (1) cowboys lived. - **(2)** must have been delayed - **(3)** would be launched - **(4)** would be flying - **(5)** the new shopping centre was. - **(6)** needn't have called - **(7)** the following day. - **(8)** should have let me know - **(9)** didn't have to save - **(10)** 3 years before and had been growing.

d) He told me : "**(1)** I worked for 2 years... **(2)** before I was transferred to the New York headquarters." - "**(3)** Why did you have your boyfriend murdered ?" he asked her. - "**(4)** What a very elegant suit my boss is wearing today," she thought. - "**(5)** You shouldn't get / It's wrong to get upset about little things," they told her. - "**(6)** Let's do our Christmas shopping..." she suggested. - "**(7)** You'd better tell them the truth," my friend answered when I asked her what to do. - She wondered : "**(8)** Has he had the measles immunisation or not ?" - She advised him : "**(9)** You should return the wallet **(10)** you found to the police station. - "**(11)** I have been trying to reach you for the last three days," he told his real estate agent. - "**(12)** Run down to the shop on the corner, **(13)** get me a dozen eggs and don't break them," she ordered him. - "**(14)** How long have you been taking violin lessons ?" she wanted to know. - The clerk told him : "**(15)** You needn't bring / don't have to bring the forms back before next week". - He

LE DISCOURS INDIRECT

explained : "**(16)** When I go to College, **(17)** I will share an apartment with a room-mate." - She often said : "**(18)** I wish **(19)** I could go hang-gliding." - "**(20)** I'm sorry for being nosy" she apologized.

e) **(1)** A youngster asked his aged granny why she kept reading her Bible all day long. **(2)** She answered that he might say **(3)** she was cramming for her final examinations.

(4) A hypocritical Boston tycoon once told Mark Twain that before he died **(5)** he meant to make a pilgrimage to the top of Mount Sinai in the Holy Land, and read the Ten Commandments aloud. **(6)** Twain suggested he (should) stay right home in Boston and keep them.

(7) Mrs Beamish called to her husband and said that the year before they had sent her mother a chair. **(8)** She asked him what he thought **(9)** they ought to do for her that year. **(10)** Mr Beamish called back and told her to electrify it.

(11) A doctor warned an ageing star that he thought **(12)** she ought to stop taking sleeping pills every night **(13)** because they were habit-forming. **(14)** She told him not to be a drip. **(15)** She had been taking them these last 20 years **(16)** and they hadn't become a habit yet.

A housewife complained constantly to her husband about the apartment they lived in. **(17)** She said that all their friends lived ten times better than they did **(18)** and that they simply had to move into a more expensive neighbourhood. **(19)** One night her long-suffering husband came home and told her that they didn't have to move after all. **(20)** The landlord had just doubled their rent.

21. LE GROUPE VERBAL : RÉVISION GÉNÉRALE

a) **(1)** has become - **(2)** knew - **(3)** have finished - **(4)** getting - **(5)** fell - **(6)** may have/ can have - **(7)** can't have - **(8)** had lost - **(9)** will be - **(10)** should (could/ may) have known - **(11)** was thinking - **(12)** had to - **(13)** had been treating / treated - **(14)** wouldn't have run away - **(15)** becomes - **(16)** struck - **(17)** achieving - **(18)** has been operating - **(19)** will have to - **(20)** may be / will be disrupted.

b) **(1)** has begun - **(2)** disappears - **(3)** is accelerating - **(4)** is - **(5)** will have vanished - **(6)** predicted - **(7)** will heave - **(8)** will drive - **(9)** used - **(10)** to nail - **(11)** has dreamed - **(12)** providing - **(13)** started - **(14)** have faced - **(15)** died - **(16)** are - **(17)** are often associated - **(18)** have been contributing - **(19)** are bickering - **(20)** to integrate.

c) **(1)** has become - **(2)** calls - **(3)** riding - **(4)** chose - **(5)** sought - **(6)** have had - **(7)** went up - **(8)** costs - **(9)** makes - **(10)** is - **(11)** has never been properly modernized - **(12)** was built - **(13)** remembers - **(14)** killed - **(15)** have neglected - **(16)** To protest - **(17)** have staged - **(18)** should take - **(19)** may / might find - **(20)** has actually fallen.

d) **(i)** - **(1)** c - **(2)** e - **(3)** a - **(4)** b - **(5)** d.
   (ii) **(1)** b - **(2)** - d - **(3)** a - **(4)** e - **(5)** c.

e) **(1)** Have you ever been to Ireland ? - **(2)** The older he became, the balder (be became). - **(3)** You must look after this child (this child must be looked after). - **(4)** Did you ask him / her what she / he had been doing for an hour ? - **(5)** You shouldn't eat so much meat. - **(6)** My car was stolen. - **(7)** Why did you have your hair cut ? - **(8)** I don't know how much this book costs. - **(9)** He helped a blind man cross the street. - **(10)** This shop might be closed.

f) **(1)** You needn't hurry (up). - **(2)** She hasn't understood what you told her, neither have I. - **(3)** Don't expect her to be on time. - **(4)** He behaves as if he were the boss. - **(5)** It's a long time since it snowed in winter / It hasn't snowed in winter for a long time. - **(6)** When she was in Japan, she never got used to eating raw fish. - **(7)** You're not listening to me, what are you thinking about ? - **(8)** What do you want to do when you are older / What do you want to be when you grow up ? - **(9)** He must have been surprised at the warm welcome he was given . - **(10)** He may have already sent off his film to be developed.

22. LES PRÉPOSITIONS

A. LES PRÉPOSITIONS DE LIEU

(1) on - (2) on - (3) throughout - (4) out of - (5) up to - (6) through - (7) into / onto - (8) Above - (9) on - (10) out of - (11) into - (12) through - (13) onto - (14) through - (15) Across - (16) from - (17) at - (18) from - (19) along - (20) over.

B. AUTRES PRÉPOSITIONS

a) (1) on - (2) to - (3) ∅ - (4) on - (5) from - (6) from - (7) in - (8) ∅ - (9) to - (10) ∅ - (11) into - (12) from - (13) to - (14) ∅ - (15) after - (16) on - (17) into - (18) of - (19) ∅ - (20) for - (21) on - (22) ∅ - (23) ∅ - (24) on - (25) in.

b) (1) by - (2) for - (3) in - (4) through - (5) with - (6) on - (7) for - (8) from - (9) in - (10) to - (11) to - (12) on - (13) from / in - (14) within - (15) for - (16) to - (17) to / in - (18) to / for - (19) on - (20) ∅ - (21) by - (22) in / in - (23) on - (24) for - (25) ∅.

c) (1) D'un coup de pied il ouvrit la porte. - (2) Tu ne peux pas aller à pied au drug-store, c'est trop loin. Tu ferais mieux d'y aller en voiture. - (3) A force de discussions, il l'a persuadée de prendre des leçons d'escrime avec lui. - (4) Il a été tué d'un coup de poignard dans une rue déserte de Chicago. - (5) Elle pressa complètement le citron, puis ajouta de l'eau et du sucre. - (6) J'avais un terrible mal de tête, une bonne nuit (sieste) m'en a débarrassé (m'a remis d'aplomb). -

(7) Ne traversez jamais une rue en courant. - **(8)** A grands coups de coudes il se fraya un chemin à travers la foule. - **(9)** Les scouts ont descendu le Colorado en canoë. - **(10)** A grands éclats de rire, ils ont chassé le fantôme de la maison.

d) **(1)** Don't lean out of the window. - **(2)** I don't like to drink out of somebody else's glass. - **(3)** What's your bag made of ? Leather ? - **(4)** Take your hands out of your pockets. - **(5)** How would you translate this expression into English ? - **(6)** Help yourself to some fruit. - **(7)** I'll buy myself a sandwich on the train. - **(8)** Do come on in. - **(9)** What floor do you live on ? - **(10)** She lives on a ranch in Texas.

23. LES MOTS DE LIAISON

a) (1) Once - (2) when - (3) so as to - (4) Whether - (5) No sooner - (6) As far as - (7) No matter - (8) Hardly - (9) even if - (10) Unless - (11) While - (12) la solution qui ne convient pas : though - (13) until - (14) in case - (15) in order to - (16) for fear that - (17) Even though - (18) whereas - (19) provided - (20) as.

b) (1) No sooner had he got the star role in a horror film than he became very rich and very famous. - (2) Although he came back quite late, dinner was waiting for him on the table. - (3) We might decide to rent this big house provided the price isn't too high. - (4) The Americans dropped an atomic bomb on Hiroshima in order to get the Japanese to surrender. - (5) Whenever they are together they always get into big arguments. - (6) The general public won't pay much attention to ecological problems until a serious accident occurs. - (7) Let me have your phone number so that I can get in touch with you. - (8) American comics have traditionally been written for children whereas French comics are read by adults as well. - (9) Hardly had the clock struck twelve when Cinderella's coach vanished into thin air. - (10) As he had come down with flu, he had to stay in bed for a week.

c) (1) unless (c) - (2) while (e) - (3) until (a) - (4) as soon as (b) - (5) so as not to (d) - (6) although (g) - (7) whereas (j) - (8) whenever (f) - (9) provided (h) - (10) for fear (i).

24. LES NOMBRES

a) **(1)** forty - **(2)** one / a hundred and thirteen - **(3)** two hundred and six - **(4)** seven hundred and fifty - **(5)** three thousand, five hundred - **(6)** ninety thousand and two - **(7)** thirty thousand, six hundred - **(8)** five hundred and eighty-two thousand, seven hundred and thirty - **(9)** a / one billion - **(10)** nineteen eighty-nine - **(11)** one billion, eight million - **(12)** nineteen eighty-five - **(13)** fifteen thousand percent - **(14)** zero point seven percent / nought point seven percent - **(15)** Elizabeth the first - **(16)** Henry the eighth - **(17)** sixteen O three - **(18)** sixth - **(19)** two thirds - **(20)** eighties.

b) **(1)** eight fifteen - **(2)** World War Two / the Second World War - **(3)** fifth - **(4)** nought / zero degrees centigrade / Celsius - **(5)** the fifteenth / fifteenth (US) - **(6)** nineteen ninety - **(7)** fourteen point three billion dollars - **(8)** two one two, seven three two, six 0, double five / six zero five five (US) - **(9)** twelve forty-nine - **(10)** one double 0 two four - **(11)** seven hundred and fifty million - **(12)** fifties - **(13)** sixties - **(14)** four hundred and fifty thousand - **(15)** fifty percent - **(16)** two thousand - **(17)** five three two, seven one eight Y - **(18)** twenty-first - **(19)** three hundred thousand - **(20)** the twelfth / twelfth (US).

25. HANDLE WITH CARE !

A. TO MAKE - TO DO

a) (1) do - (2) do - (3) doing - (4) make - (5) make - (6) make - (7) make - (8) make - (9) do - (10) do - (11) make - (12) do - (13) (will) make - (14) do - (15) will do - (16) making - (17) are doing - (18) make - (19) are doing - (20) doing - (21) make - (22) makes - (23) To make - (24) make - (25) to do.

b) (1) had made - (2) say - (3) had - (4) do - (5) make - (6) Let - (7) made - (8) get - (9) show - (10) are giving.

c) (i) (1) b - (2) c - (3) d - (4) e - (5) a.
(ii) (1) b - (2) d - (3) a - (4) e - (5) c.

B. TO SAY - TO TELL

(1) has often been said / is often said - (2) say - (3) tell - (4) To tell - (5) say - (6) tell - (7) to tell - (8) tell - (9) wouldn't tell - (10) to say - (11) to tell - (12) said - (13) to say - (14) tells - (15) said - (16) to say - (17) told - (18) said - (19) says - (20) unsaid.

C. LES FAUX-AMIS

a) (1) relatives - (2) soon - (3) considered - (4) a path for carts and carriages - (5) talented - (6) petty - (7) finally - (8) compassion - (9) It was evident that she was trying to cheat me. - (10) doubt the fact.

b) (1) Nowadays, drug-addiction is actually on the rise in many European countries (om: today) — (2) She keeps

HANDLE WITH CARE ! 199

her diary in the bottom drawer of her desk (om: study) - **(3)** Your train will be leaving from platform number 3 (om: quay) - **(4)** He is the best cook this restaurant has had in a long time (om: cooker) - **(5)** She always buys her books second-hand in the little book-shop down the street (om: library) - **(6)** Robert Louis Stevenson's nickname was "Velvet coat" because he liked to wear an old velvet jacket (om: surname) - **(7)** She was too busy to be sensitive to the needs of her children (om: sensible) - **(8)** As she had hoped her son would make his way in Hollywood, she was left with a strong feeling of disappointment (om: deception) - **(9)** Some American towns are experimenting with curfews for the young to keep them off the streets after 10 (om: experiencing) - **(10)** The publisher has not sent me all the books I had ordered (om: editor).

c) **(1)** How much does her husband earn (make) a month ? I absolutely don't know (I have no idea). - **(2)** Yesterday I listened to a very good dramatization (version) of one of Faulkner's short-stories on the radio. - **(3)** She took her exam and passed. - **(4)** I was given a (Brit) cine-camera / (US) movie-camera for my birthday. — **(5)** He works for an advertising agency. - **(6)** The prehistoric caves in Lascaux are known all over the world / in the whole world. - **(7)** Industrialization has often taken place regardless of damage to the environment and to the general health of the population. - **(8)** Cinderella lived in poverty in the shadow of her sisters who made her miserable. - **(9)** He asked me where the nearest RER station was and at what stop he should get off. - **(10)** His new film got very warm reviews from the critics in the film industry.

d) (1) Et si tu descendais rapidement chez le marchand de vins pour acheter une bouteille de liqueur pour ton grand-père. (liquor-store : US - off-licence : GB) - **(2)** Quand elle le vit elle fit comme si elle ne le connaissait pas et ne lui prêta aucune attention. - **(3)** Ses voisins la considèrent comme une jeune femme tout à fait comme il faut mais très dépensière. - **(4)** Si une nouvelle crise du pétrole devait avoir lieu, les pays occidentaux pourraient bien avoir à affronter une augmentation du prix de l'essence. - **(5)** Des deux sœurs, c'est Mary Ann qui a la plus jolie silhouette. - **(6)** Elle envoya les enfants dans le jardin parce qu'ils l'irritaient. - **(7)** J'ai perdu la pellicule que j'ai achetée ce matin. - **(8)** Beaucoup de gens ont des préjugés envers les Tsiganes. - **(9)** En raison de la crise économique, le directeur n'a pas pu satisfaire aux exigences de ces ouvriers. - **(10)** ''Nous avons commencé à nous disputer et ensuite il m'a injuriée'' dit-elle en pleurant.

26. AMÉRICANISMES

a) **(1)** fall - **(2)** doing the dishes - **(3)** apartment - **(4)** cleaning-lady - **(5)** elevator - **(6)** first-floor - **(7)** gas-station - **(8)** truck - **(9)** parking-lot - **(10)** shopping-cart - **(11)** cans - **(12)** cookies - **(13)** chips - **(14)** candy - **(15)** T-bone steak - **(16)** check-out counter - **(17)** stand in line - **(18)** trunk - **(19)** after - **(20)** movies.

b) **(1)** freezer - **(2)** broken into - **(3)** two-floored - **(4)** holiday - **(5)** lay - **(6)** wing - **(7)** hoovers - **(8)** handbag - **(9)** pavement - **(10)** trainers.

c) **(1)** What colour are letter-boxes in the United States ? (om: mail-boxes). - **(2)** Sorry, Madam, I can't put your call through at the moment, the line is busy. (om: engaged). - **(3)** Have you seen the famous British film called *My beautiful launderette* ? (om: laundromat). - **(4)** You will find the sugar-bowl on the bottom shelf in the kitchen cupboard. (om: closet). - **(5)** The most successful scene of the film takes place in the carriage of a crowded train. (om: car).

d) **(1)** chips - **(2)** dustbin - **(3)** rubber - **(4)** railway - **(5)** holiday-makers - **(6)** tube - **(7)** police-vans - **(8)** windscreen - **(9)** reverse charges - **(10)** number plates.

LISTE DES VERBES IRRÉGULIERS

Les américanismes sont indiqués par *. Les formes peu courantes, archaïques ou littéraires sont données entre parenthèses. Les traductions ci-dessous ne sont pas restrictives et ne donnent qu'un des sens de base.

infinitif		prétérit	participe passé
abide	*(supporter)*	(abode) [1]	abided
arise	*(surgir)*	arose	arisen
awake	*(s'éveiller)*	awoke, awaked	awoken, (awaked)
bear	*(porter)*	bore	borne [2]
beat	*(battre)*	beat	beaten [3]
become	*(devenir)*	became	become
befall	*(arriver)*	befell	befallen
beget	*(engendrer)*	begot	begotten
begin	*(commencer)*	began	begun
behold	*(apercevoir)*	beheld	beheld
bend	*(courber)*	bent	bent [4]
bereave	*(priver)*	bereaved	bereft [5]
beseech	*(implorer)*	besought	besought
bestride	*(chevaucher)*	bestrode	bestridden
bet	*(parier)*	bet, betted	bet, betted
bid	*(offrir)*	bid	bid
bid	*(commander)*	bade	bidden
bind	*(attacher)*	bound	bound
bite	*(mordre)*	bit	bitten
bleed	*(saigner)*	bled	bled
blow	*(souffler)*	blew	blown
break	*(casser)*	broke	broken [6]
breed	*(élever)*	bred	bred

VERBES IRREGULIERS

bring	*(apporter)*	brought	brought
broadcast	*(diffuser)*	broadcast	broadcast
build	*(construire)*	built	built
burn	*(brûler)*	burnt, burned	burnt, burned
burst	*(éclater)*	burst	burst
buy	*(acheter)*	bought	bought
cast	*(jeter)*	cast	cast
catch	*(attraper)*	caught	caught
chide	*(gronder)*	chid, chided	chid, (chidden), chided
choose	*(choisir)*	chose	chosen
cleave	*(fendre)*	clove, cleft, cleaved	cloven, cleft [7]
cleave	*(adhérer)*	cleaved, (clave)	cleaved
cling	*(s'accrocher à)*	clung	clung
clothe	*(habiller)*	clothed, (clad)	clothed, (clad)
come	*(venir)*	came	come
cost	*(coûter)*	cost	cost
creep	*(ramper)*	crept	crept
crow	*(chanter)*	crowed, (crew)	crowed
cut	*(couper)*	cut	cut
dare	*(oser)*	dared, (durst)	dared, (durst)
deal	*(traiter)*	dealt	dealt
dig	*(fouiller)*	dug	dug
dive	*(plonger)*	dived, dove*	dived
draw	*(dessiner, tirer)*	drew	drawn
dream	*(rêver)*	dreamt, dreamed	dreamt, dreamed
drink	*(boire)*	drank	drunk [8]
drive	*(conduire)*	drove	driven
dwell	*(demeurer)*	dwelt, dwelled	dwelt, dwelled
eat	*(manger)*	ate	eaten
fall	*(tomber)*	fell	fallen
feed	*(nourrir)*	fed	fed
feel	*(sentir)*	felt	felt
fight	*(battre)*	fought	fought
find	*(trouver)*	found	found
fit	*(aller à)*	fit*, fitted	fit*, fitted
flee	*(s'envoler)*	fled	fled
fling	*(lancer)*	flung	flung
fly	*(voler)*	flew	flown
forbear	*(s'abstenir)*	forbore	forborne

VERBES IRREGULIERS 205

forbid	*(interdire)*	forbad(e)	forbidden
forget	*(oublier)*	forgot	forgotten
forgive	*(pardonner)*	forgave	forgiven
forsake	*(abandonner)*	forsook	forsaken
freeze	*(geler)*	froze	frozen
get	*(obtenir)*	got	got, gotten* [9]
gild	*(dorer)*	gilt, gilded	gilt, gilded [10]
gird	*(ceindre)*	girt, girded	girt, girded [10]
give	*(donner)*	gave	given
go	*(aller)*	went	gone
grind	*(grincer)*	ground	ground
grow	*(pousser)*	grew	grown
hang	*(pendre)*	hung, hanged [11]	hung, hanged [11]
hear	*(entendre)*	heard	heard
heave	*(lever)*	hove, heaved [12]	hove, heaved [12]
hew	*(tailler)*	hewed	hewn, hewed
hide	*(cacher)*	hid	hidden
hit	*(frapper)*	hit	hit
hold	*(tenir)*	held	held
hurt	*(blesser)*	hurt	hurt
keep	*(garder)*	kept	kept
kneel	*(s'agenouiller)*	knelt, kneeled	knelt, kneeled
knit	*(tricoter)*	knit, knitted [13]	knit, knitted [13]
know	*(savoir, connaître)*	knew	known
lay	*(coucher)*	laid	laid
lead	*(mener)*	led	led
lean	*(s'appuyer)*	leant, leaned	leant, leaned
leap	*(sauter)*	leapt, leaped	leapt, leaped
learn	*(apprendre)*	learnt, learned	learnt, learned
leave	*(laisser)*	left	left
lend	*(prêter)*	lent	lent
let	*(laisser)*	let	let
lie	*(coucher)*	lay	lain
light	*(allumer)*	lit, lighted	lit, lighted [14]
lose	*(perdre)*	lost	lost
make	*(faire)*	made	made
mean	*(signifier)*	meant	meant
meet	*(rencontrer)*	met	met
melt	*(fondre)*	melted	melted, molten [15]
mow	*(faucher)*	mowed	mown, mowed

pay	*(payer)*	paid	paid
plead	*(plaider)*	pled*, pleaded	pled*, pleaded [16]
put	*(poser)*	put	put
quit	*(quitter)*	quit, (quitted)	quit, (quitted) [17]
read	*(lire)*	read	read
rend	*(déchirer)*	rent	rent
rid	*(débarasser)*	rid, (ridded)	rid
ride	*(monter à)*	rode	ridden
ring	*(sonner)*	rang	rung
rise	*(se lever)*	rose	risen
run	*(courir)*	ran	run
saw	*(scier)*	sawed	sawn, sawed
say	*(dire)*	said	said
see	*(voir)*	saw	seen
seek	*(chercher)*	sought	sought
sell	*(vendre)*	sold	sold
send	*(envoyer)*	sent	sent
set	*(mettre)*	set	set
sew	*(coudre)*	sewed	sewn, sewed
shake	*(secouer)*	shook	shaken
shear	*(tondre)*	sheared	shorn, sheared [18]
shed	*(perdre)*	shed	shed
shine	*(briller)*	shone	shone [19]
shoe	*(chausser)*	shod, shoed	shod, shoed [20]
shoot	*(abattre, tirer)*	shot	shot
show	*(montrer)*	showed	shown, showed
shrink	*(rétrécir)*	shrank, shrunk	shrunk, shrunken [21]
shut	*(fermer)*	shut	shut
sing	*(chanter)*	sang	sung
sink	*(couler)*	sank	sunk, sunken [22]
sit	*(s'asseoir)*	sat	sat
slay	*(tuer)*	slew	slain
sleep	*(dormir)*	slept	slept
slide	*(glisser)*	slid	slid
sling	*(lancer)*	slung	slung
slink	*(s'en aller furtivement)*	slunk	slunk
slit	*(fendre)*	slit	slit
smell	*(sentir)*	smelt, smelled	smelt, smelled
smite	*(frapper)*	smote	smitten [23]

VERBES IRREGULIERS

sneak	*(entrer, etc. à la dérobée)*	snuck*, sneaked	snuck*, sneaked
sow	*(semer)*	sowed	sown, sowed
speak	*(parler)*	spoke	spoken
speed	*(aller vite)*	sped, speeded	sped, speeded
spell	*(écrire)*	spelt, spelled	spelt, spelled
spend	*(dépenser)*	spent	spent
spill	*(renverser)*	spilt, spilled	spilt, spilled
spin	*(filer)*	spun	spun
spit	*(cracher)*	spat, spit*	spat, spit*
split	*(se briser)*	split	split
spoil	*(abîmer)*	spoilt, spoiled	spoilt, spoiled
spread	*(étendre)*	spread	spread
spring	*(bondir)*	sprang	sprung
stand	*(se tenir)*	stood	stood
steal	*(voler)*	stole	stolen
stick	*(enfoncer, coller)*	stuck	stuck
sting	*(piquer)*	stung	stung
stink	*(puer)*	stank	stunk
strew	*(répandre)*	strewed	strewn, strewed
stride	*(avancer à grands pas)*	strode	stridden
strike	*(frapper)*	struck	struck, stricken [24]
string	*(enfiler)*	strung	strung
strive	*(s'efforcer)*	strove	striven
swear	*(jurer)*	swore	sworn
sweat	*(suer)*	sweat*, sweated	sweat*, sweated
sweep	*(balayer)*	swept	swept
swell	*(gonfler)*	swelled	swollen, swelled [25]
swim	*(nager)*	swam	swum
swing	*(se balancer)*	swung	swung
take	*(prendre)*	took	taken
teach	*(enseigner)*	taught	taught
tear	*(déchirer)*	tore	torn
tell	*(dire)*	told	told
think	*(penser)*	thought	thought
thrive	*(fleurir)*	thrived, (throve)	thrived, (thriven)
throw	*(jeter)*	threw	thrown
thrust	*(pousser)*	thrust	thrust
tread	*(marcher)*	trod	trodden

understand	(comprendre)	understood	understood
undertake	(s'engager)	undertook	undertaken
wake	(se réveiller)	woke, waked	woken, waked
wear	(porter)	wore	worn
weave	(tisser)	wove [26]	woven [26]
weep	(pleurer)	wept	wept
wet	(mouiller)	wet*, wetted [27]	wet*, wetted [27]
win	(gagner)	won	won
wind	(remonter)	wound	wound
wring	(tordre)	wrung	wrung
write	(écrire)	wrote	written

(1) Régulier dans la construction **abide by** "se conformer à, suivre" : **they abided by the rules**.

(2) Mais **born** au passif = "né" ou comme un adjectif : **he was born in France/a born gentleman**.

(3) Remarquez la forme familière **this has me beat/you have me beat there** *cela me dépasse/tu m'as posé une colle* et **beat** dans le sens de "très fatigué, épuisé" : **I am (dead) beat**.

(4) Remarquez la phrase **on one's bended knees** *à genoux*.

(5) Mais **bereaved** dans le sens de "endeuillé" comme dans **the bereaved received no compensation** *la famille du disparu ne reçut aucune compensation*. Comparez : **he was bereft of speech** *il en perdit la parole*.

(6) Mais **broke** quand il s'agit d'un adjectif = "fauché" : **I'm broke**.

(7) **cleft** n'est employé qu'avec le sens de "coupé en deux". Remarquez **cleft palate** *palais fendu* et **(to be caught) in a cleft stick** *(être) dans une impasse*, mais **cloven foot/hoof** *sabot fendu*.

(8) Quand c'est un adjectif placé avant le nom, **drunken** "ivre, ivrogne" est parfois employé (**a lot of drunk(en) people** *beaucoup de gens ivres*) et il **doit** toujours être employé devant les noms représentant des objets inanimés (**one of his**

VERBES IRREGULIERS

usual drunken parties *une de ses soirées habituelles où l'on boit*).

(9) Mais **have got to** se dit aussi en américain avec le sens de "devoir, être obligé de" : **a man has got to do what a man has got to do** *un homme doit faire ce qu'il doit faire*. Comparez avec : **she has gotten into a terrible mess** *elle s'est fourrée dans une sale situation*.

(10) Les formes du participe passé **gilt** et **girt** sont très couramment employées comme adjectif placé avant le nom : **gilt mirrors** *des miroirs dorés*, **a flower-girt grave** *une tombe entourée de fleurs* (mais toujours **gilded youth** *la jeunesse dorée*, dans lequel **gilded** signifie "riche et bienheureux").

(11) Régulier quand il a le sens de "mettre à mort par pendaison".

(12) **Hove** est employé dans le domaine nautique comme dans la phrase **heave into sight** : **just then Mary hove into sight** *et Mary pointa à l'horizon/apparut*.

(13) Irrégulier quand il a le sens de "unir" (**a close-knit family** *une famille unie*), mais régulier lorsqu' il a le sens de "fabriquer en laine" et quand il fait référence aux os — "se souder".

(14) Lorsque le participe passé est employé comme un adjectif devant un nom, **lighted** est souvent préféré à **lit** : **a lighted match** *une allumette allumée* (mais : **the match is lit, she has lit a match** *l'allumette est allumée, elle a allumé l'allumette*). Dans les noms composés, on emploie généralement **lit** : **well-lit streets** *des rues bien éclairées*. Au sens figuré (avec **up**) **lit** uniquement est employé au prétérit et au participe passé : **her face lit up when she saw me** *son visage s'illumina lorsqu'elle me vit*.

(15) On emploie **molten** uniquement comme un adjectif devant les noms, et seulement lorsqu'il signifie "fondu à une très haute température", par exemple : **molten lead** *du plomb fondu* (mais **melted butter** *du beurre fondu*).

(16) En anglais d'Ecosse et en américain, on emploie **pled** au passé et au participe passé.

(17) En américain, les formes régulières ne sont pas employées, et elles sont de plus en plus rares en anglais britannique.

(18) Le participe passé est normalement **shorn** devant un nom (**newly-shorn lambs** *des agneaux tout juste tondus*) et toujours dans la phrase (**to be**) **shorn of** *(être) privé de* : **shorn of his riches he was nothing** *privé de ses richesses, il n'était plus rien*.

(19) Mais régulier quand il a le sens de "cirer, astiquer" en américain.

(20) Quand c'est un adjectif, on n'emploie que **shod** : **a well-shod foot** *un pied bien chaussé*.

(21) **Shrunken** n'est employé que lorsqu'il est adjectif : **shrunken limbs/her face was shrunken** *des membres rabougris/son visage était ratatiné*.

(22) **Sunken** n'est employé que comme un adjectif : **sunken eyes** *des yeux creux*.

(23) Verbe archaïque dont le participe passé **smitten** s'emploie encore comme adjectif : **he's completely smitten with her** *il est complètement fou d'elle*.

(24) **Stricken** n'est utilisé que dans le sens figuré (**a stricken family/stricken with poverty** *une famille accablée/accablée par la pauvreté*). Il est très courant dans les noms composés (accablé par) : **poverty-stricken, fever-stricken, horror-stricken** (aussi **horror-struck**), **terror-stricken** (aussi **terror-struck**), mais on dit toujours **thunderstruck** *frappé par la surprise, abasourdi de surprise*.

C'est aussi un emploi américain **the remark was stricken from the record** *la remarque a été rayée du procès-verbal*.

VERBES IRRÉGULIERS

(25) **Swollen** est plus courant que **swelled** comme verbe (**her face has swollen** *son visage est gonflé*) et comme adjectif (**her face is swollen/a swollen face**). **A swollen head** *une grosse tête*, pour quelqu'un qui a une haute opinion de soi-même, devient **a swelled head** en américain.

(26) Mais il est régulier lorsqu'il a le sens de "se faufiler" : **the motorbike weaved elegantly through the traffic** *la moto se faufila avec élégance dans la circulation.*

(27) Mais irrégulier aussi en anglais britannique lorsqu'il a le sens de "mouiller par de l'urine" : **he wet his bed again last night** *il a encore mouillé son lit la nuit dernière.*

50 famous English proverbs

chosen by Anthony Burgess

all's well that ends well
 tout est bien qui finit bien
all's fair in love and war
 en amour, la ruse est de bonne guerre
all that glitters is not gold
 tout ce qui brille n'est pas or
as well be hanged for a sheep as for a lamb
 autant vaut être pendu pour un mouton que pour un agneau
beggars can't be choosers
 ne choisit pas qui emprunte
better late than never
 mieux vaut tard que jamais
a bird in the hand is worth two in the bush
 un tiens vaut mieux que deux tu l'auras
birds of a feather flock together
 qui se ressemble s'assemble

blood is thicker than water
  nous sommes unis par la voix, la force, du sang

charity begins at home
  charité bien ordonnée commence par soi(-même)

discretion is the better part of valour
  l'essentiel du courage, c'est la prudence

don't count your chickens before they are hatched
  il ne faut pas vendre la peau de l'ours avant de l'avoir tué

don't put all your eggs in one basket
  il ne faut pas mettre tous ses œufs dans le même panier

don't wash your dirty linen in public
  il faut laver son linge sale en famille

an Englishman's home is his castle
  charbonnier est maître chez soi

enough is as good as a feast
  assez vaut (un) festin

every cloud has a silver lining
  dans toute chose il y a un bon côté

every little helps
  on fait feu de tout bois

ENGLISH PROVERBS

familiarity breeds contempt
  la familiarité engendre, fait naître, le mépris

first come first served
  les premiers vont devant

forgive and forget
  il faut oublier et pardonner

God helps him who helps himself
  aide-toi, le ciel t'aidera

half a loaf is better than no bread
  faute de grives, on mange des merles

he who pays the piper calls the tune
  qui paye a bien le droit de choisir

if the cap fits, wear it!
  qui se sent morveux se mouche!

it is an ill wind that blows nobody any good
  à quelque chose malheur est bon

it's no use crying over spilt milk
  à chose faite point de remède

least said soonest mended
  moins on en parle, mieux cela vaut

live and let live
  il faut que tout le monde vive

look before you leap
  il faut réfléchir avant d'agir

216 ENGLISH PROVERBS

many hands make light work
 à plusieurs mains, l'ouvrage avance

more haste less speed
 plus on se hâte moins on avance

necessity is the mother of invention
 nécessité est mère de l'invention

never look a gift horse in the mouth
 à cheval donné on ne regarde pas à la bride

no news is good news
 point de nouvelles, bonnes nouvelles

once bitten twice shy
 chat échaudé craint l'eau froide

one man's meat is another man's poison
 ce qui guérit l'un tue l'autre

people who live in glass houses shouldn't throw stones
 il faut être sans défauts pour critiquer autrui

the proof of the pudding is in the eating
 à l'œuvre on connaît l'artisan

the road to hell is paved with good intentions
 l'enfer est pavé de bonnes intentions

ENGLISH PROVERBS

there are none so deaf as those that will not hear
il n'est pire sourd que celui qui ne veut pas entendre

too many cooks spoil the broth
trop de cuisinières gâtent la sauce

two's company, three's a crowd
deux s'amusent, trois s'embêtent

when in Rome do as the Romans do
il faut hurler avec les loups

while the cat's away the mice (will) play
quand le chat n'est pas là, les souris dansent

you cannot make a silk purse out of a sow's ear
on ne saurait faire d'une buse un épervier

you can't have your cake and eat it
on ne peut pas avoir le drap et l'argent

one swallow doesn't make a summer
une hirondelle ne fait pas le printemps

a stitch in time saves nine
un point à temps en épargne cent

it never rains but it pours
 un malheur, un bonheur, ne vient
 jamais seul

INDEX

a, an 9-10, 12-13
above 129
across 85-90, 129
actual, actually 147
adjectifs composés 29-30, 32-34
adjectifs indéfinis 40-46
adjectifs de nationalité 31
adjectifs numéraux 33-34
adjectifs possessifs 24
adjectifs substantivés 32-34
adresses 141
adverbes 47-50
after 73, 76
again 49
âge 99
ago 65-69
all, all too 43, 46
almost 48
already 48, 50
also 47
although 137-138
always 47
américanismes 150-153
années 140
another 45
any et composés 40-46
apposition 10
article défini 10-13
article indéfini 9-13
as 135, 139
as far as 135-139
as long as 135-139
as soon as 123, 135-139
at 129
auxiliaires 91-96
auxiliaires modaux 77-84
away 85-90

be able to 79-84
be about to 54, 70-72, 91

be allowed to 79-84
be born 99
be bound to 57, 71
be going to 70-72
be like 100
be to 71, 84, 118
been 63
before 49, 57, 119, 121
best 28
better 28-29, 32-34
both 43
but (expression du) 105, 107
but 94-96
by + ing 55
by + passif 113-116
by (autres) 82, 131, 133, 140

can, cannot, can't 77-84, 123
can't help 51
can't stand 56, 110
cas possessif 23-26
causatifs 51, 53, 57, 93, 101-103, 107-110, 114, 116, 120
ce que, ce qui 39
comparaison 27-29, 32-34
conditionnel présent 73-76
conditionnel passé 74-76
conjonctions de subordination 135-139
could 74-76, 77-84

dare 67
dates 140-143
degrés de comparaison 27-29, 32-34
devoir 84
discours direct 120
discours indirect 117-119, 121-122
do (auxiliaire) 91-96
do (auxiliaire emphatique) 68

do et *make* 142-144
dont/ce dont 39
doubles comparatifs 27-29, 32-34
down 85-90
due to 84

each 42, 44
each other 35-36
either 43, 50, 94-96
either ... or 44
elder, eldest 33
en + **participe présent** 58
enough 41, 42, 47, 105
ever 49, 50
every 43
everybody, everyone 43
everything 43
exclamation 111-112
expect 53
except 52, 107-110, 127

faire faire 101-103
far 49
faux-amis 146-149
few, a few 41
first 100
for 52, 54, 65-69, 85-90, 131, 132, 133
for fear that 135-139
fractions 140
from 129, 130, 132
futur antérieur 70-72
futur progressif 70-72
futur simple 70-72

gérondif 51-58
get somebody to do something 54, 55, 101
get used to 52, 57, 76
go, gone 63

had better 57, 83, 93, 107-110
hardly 48, 49, 50, 92, 95, 135-139

have been, have gone 63
have to 79-84, 91, 93
here 50
hers 24
herself 36
how 97, 98, 99
how big 99
how far 97
how high 98
how long (durée) 66-69, 97, 98
how long ago 66-69, 98
how many 97, 98, 99
how much 98, 99
how often 84
how old 85
how tall 85
how to 57, 125
however 135-139
hundred 34

I'd like 51, 57, 107-110
if 73-76, 126, 127
in (lieu) 129
in (temps) 67
in case + should 136
in order to 136
in spite of 135-139
infinitif 51-58
into 85-90, 129
inversion 48-49, 106
itself 36

jours 24
just 113

latest 28
least 28-33
lest 135-139
let + infinitif 51, 107
let's + infinitif 92
likely (to be) 57, 83
little, a little 41
look like 99
lot, a lot, lots of 41-42

INDEX 221

made of 134
make et *do* 142-144
manage to 53, 56
many 41, 42
may 77-84, 123
mesures 140-141
might 75, 77, 84
million 33
modaux 77-84
mois 141
most 28, 43, 44
mots de liaison 135-139
much 41-42
must 77-84
mustn't 77-84
myself 36

nationalité (adjectifs) 31
nationalité (noms) 21-22
needn't 77-84, 92, 119-120
neither 44, 45, 95-96
neither ... nor 43
never 48
no 42
no matter how 135-139
no sooner ... than 106, 135-139
nobody 44
nombres 140-141
noms 15-22
noms composés 19-21
noms de nationalité 21-22
none 45
noone 44
nor 95-96
nothing 44
nought (zero) 140-141
numéros de téléphone 141

off 49, 85-89
often (how) 98
omission de l'article 10-13
omission du relatif 37-39
on 86, 129, 130, 134
once 48, 99, 135-139
one(s) 24, 44, 45

oneself 36
other 46
ought to 79-84
out 85-90
out of 129
over 87-90, 129
over with 86-87
owe 84
own (of my) 36

passé (temps du) 62-69
passif 113-116
place de l'adjectif 27
place de l'adverbe 47-48
plaques d'immatriculation 141
pluperfect 67-69, 124
pluriel 15
possessifs (adjectifs, adverbes) 24-26
possession 23-26
postpositions (particules) 85-90
pourcentages 140-141
préfixes 31-32
prépositions de lieu 129-130
prépositions (autres) 130-134
présent progressif 59-61
présent simple 59-61
present perfect simple 63-69
present perfect progressif 63-69
prétérit progressif 62-69, 124
prétérit simple 62-69
pronoms indéfinis 40-46
pronoms interrogatifs 97-100
pronoms possessifs 23-26
pronoms réfléchis et réciproques 35-36
pronoms relatifs 37-39
propositions infinitives 52, 53, 104, 105, 107-110
propositions relatives 37-39
provided 135-139

quantifieurs 40-46
questions 97-100
question-tags 91-93
quite 47

rather 48
rather (would) 51
relatifs 37-39
reprises verbales 91-96

say et *tell* 145
seldom 48
several 42, 43
shall 71, 78, 84
should 73-76, 77-84, 107
since 65-69, 135-139
since when 66-69, 99
so 93-96
so as to 135-139
so much, so many 40-41, 128
so that 135-139
some et composés 40-41
still 47, 49, 50
structures idiomatiques avec inversion 106-107
such, such a 111-112
suffixes 17-19
superlatifs 27-29, 31-34

tags de réponse 93-96
tall (how) 99
tell et *say* 145
that (relatif) 37
the 10-13
themselves 35-36
then 47
there is/was 64, 91-92, 99
there is no + gérondif 54-56
therefore 50
though 136-139
thousand 34
through 22, 85-90, 129
to 129, 134
to + gérondif 124
too 105
twice 99

unless 135-139
until 135-139

up 85-90
used (it's no) 51, 53
used to 92, 95, 98, 113

verbes composés 85-90
verbes de perception 54, 55, 57
very much (place de) 47

want 57, 104-105
well 47
were (subjonctif) 93, 128
what 37, 54
what about 56
what colour 97
what ... for 98, 99
what with 39
whatever 135-139
when 37, 97, 135-139
whenever 135-139
where 97, 98
whereas 135-139
whether 118, 127, 135-139
which 37, 97, 98
while 57, 135-139
within 132
who 37, 97, 98
whole (the) 42, 43
whom 34-36, 97, 100
whomever 38
whose 37, 97, 98
why 37, 52, 97
will 70-72, 78, 93, 96
wish 105, 107-110, 127
won't 91, 96
worse 28, 29, 32
worst 28
would 73-76
would rather 51, 52, 57, 92, 95, 108-110

yet 49, 50
yourself 36
yourselves 35

zero 141

Dans la même série :

GRAMMAIRE ANGLAISE
★ Grammaire détaillée de l'anglais d'aujourd'hui
★ Indispensable du lycée à l'université
★ Des exemples types de la vie courante

142 mm × 96 mm/256 pp/couverture plastifiée
ISBN 0 245-50078-2

VERBES ANGLAIS
★ 1 000 verbes composés avec leur définition et des exemples
★ La formation des verbes
★ L'utilisation des temps
★ Un index renvoyant aux verbes modèles

142 mm × 96 mm/256 pp/couverture plastifiée
ISBN 0245-50076-6

VOCABULAIRE ANGLAIS
★ Indispensable pour vos révisions
et pour la préparation au bac
★ 6 000 mots classés en 65 thèmes

142 mm × 96 mm/256 pp/couverture plastifiée
ISBN 0 245-50077-4